MW01711665

THE INNER SUCCESS PROJECT

Elina Lee

THE INNER SUCCESS PROJECT

The Complete 30-Day Guide to Inner-Peace, Inner-Connection, Inner-Worth, Inner-Mastery, Inner-Development, Inner-Discovery, Inner-Love.

Copyright © 2018, Elina Lee

All rights reserved. No part of this publication may be reproduced in any form or by any electronic or mechanical means, including information storage and retrieval systems, without permission in writing from the author, except by reviewers, who may quote brief passages in a review.

ISBN 978-0-5784-1865-0 (Paperback Edition)
ISBN 978-0-5784-1868-1 (E-book Edition)

Front cover image by Blythe Eland
www.blytheelandphotography.com

Printed in the United States of America
First Edition November 2018

A Plus, Produced and Directed by Jordan Zaslow. (2015). *Would You Rather Be Rich or Happy? (A Pint-Sized Social Experiment).* Retrieved October 2017, from https://youtu.be/6JBSdWD4O0Y.

Revise Sociology. (2016). *What Percentage of Your Life Will You Spend at Work?* Retrieved June 2018, from https://revisesociology.com/2016/08/16/percentage-life-work/.

www.innersuccessproject.com

I dedicate this book to *Jacob*. My best friend, business partner, and brother from another mother. Thank you for believing in me when no one else would and standing by my side to bring this vision to life. Let's go take over the world, help, heal, save, and change some lives, bruh.

#yinyanginthisthang

Contents

THE

INNER SUCCESS PROJECT

Introduction

Before you begin your 30-day journey, you should get to know me. ….

I'm Elina. I just retired from being a professional asshole, and money-driven, depressed, unhappy, unfulfilled, egotistical douchebag who spent the past decade selfishly working my ass off solely for financial gain. Let me also start off by apologizing for my not-so-lady-like language. If the "F" word offends you then you should probably just put this book down right now. If you're easily offended in general, then this probably isn't the book for you either because over the next thirty days, we're going to tap into some deep shit that will have you re-evaluating yourself, your life, your relationships, your awareness, your past, your future, and your decisions on a whole new level.

So, back to my original introduction: retired professional asshole. Don't be that person. I was young, naïve, and oblivious to the important things in life. I started my first company at age twenty and, during the past decade, I helped to build a multimillion-dollar industry from the ground up.

There's not much that's special about me or my background; I'm a high school and college dropout, arrested as an adolescent, in and out of trouble, became a mother at seventeen, no professional experience or training before my first company; just an ambitious young woman who was hungry for success and was eager to rise to the top.

What I always found so ironic and quite entertaining was that so many people thought I was this happy, successful, clean-cut, innocent business woman who had it all together but what they didn't realize (or honestly care to take the time to learn) was that I was, in fact, the complete opposite. Sure, I was successful, but I wasn't happy; and I definitely wasn't innocent.

I actually spent much of my younger years experimenting with drugs, getting expelled from schools (I, unfortunately, attended five different schools in less than a twelve-month period before I dropped out), running away from home, getting arrested, shoplifting, breaking and entering, stealing cars, getting in fights, escaping from juvenile correctional facilities; you name it, I probably did it. Preachers' kids are always the worst. (Sorry, Mom and Dad.)

So, trust me when I say this: If a fuck-up like me can become successful, find happiness, experience true love, help others, and live a fulfilled and purposeful life, then so can you.

From the outside looking in, life was good. I was young, rich, successful, and attractive. I traveled the world for my profession. Our companies produced hundreds of events in nearly ten countries and we worked with the most talented professionals within our industry. I mingled with, partied with, and met multiple celebrities. I had friends in nearly every major city of the United States and in numerous foreign countries. I signed the papers to my first home at age twenty-five. It was an 8,400 square foot water front home in a privately gated community. My son was enrolled in private school and I was married to my business partner. Sounds great, doesn't it?

It took me nearly a decade to realize that I was living life the wrong way; a decade of privately dealing with depression, anxiety, loneliness, anger, regret, resentment, pain, and a fuck ton of superficial success that wasn't worth it.

In fact, when I became uber successful and had everything I had ever thought I wanted right in my hands is right around the time that I made the conscious decision to walk away from it all to set out on my journey toward "*Inner Success.*" Insane, right? Stupid? Outrageous? What the fuck were you thinking, Elina? (Oh yeah. Trust me. I've heard it all.)

Wrong. It was the best decision I had made in my entire life. It was the hardest and most painful decision I've ever had to make but it was worth it. Every bit of it.

Sometimes, in life, you must make decisions that others won't quite understand or agree with; that's ok, you do it anyway. You do it for you. It took me years to finally gather the courage to do what I did. When I finally made the decision to act, I felt so free, so empowered, so happy; I knew I made the right decision.

I had spent the past decade feeling that I had to maintain a certain image or live my life a certain way because of how my customers, clients, and peers would view me. I felt that I had no one to turn to. I felt that no one else cared. I felt that I had to be strong for myself because no one else was present in my personal life. All in the meantime, I had to pretend to be someone I wasn't and maintain appearances for my business and public reputation. That's not living. That's not a life. That's playing a character. That's a fucking façade.

For so many years, I spent my time and effort trying to be strong for everyone else that I forgot to be strong for myself. The time had come for me to take my power back. It was time for me to have my happiness.

If you're reading this right now and you're unsure of whether or not it's your time to be happy, fulfilled, loved, and excited about your life, guess what? It's time.

You can take your power back, too. You can make your own choice; even when you feel like that's not an option. This is your life and only you have the ability to take charge of it. You just have to make the choice to do it. You have to take action. You have to step out of your comfort zone if you want a change to happen.

It took me nearly a decade to realize that happiness isn't about success, money, or fame. Happiness is found within; it's about fulfilling your passions, your talents, your self-worth, your inner-discovery, your inner-mastery, your inner-strength, and your inner-peace.

It's surrounding yourself with the people that you love the most, the people that bring out the best in you, the people that inspire you to become all that they know you can be, the people who still support you when you're at your lowest point and have absolutely nothing to offer them. That's love. That's happiness. That's fulfillment. You deserve to feel that way all the time.

Life is too short to live it to other people's standards. Don't be like me and wait a decade to take your power back. Learn from my mistakes and do something about your happiness before it's too late.

Let's start today.

1

Your Journey Awaits

"You don't have to be great to start,
but you have to start to be great."
– Zig Ziglar

Alright. Here we go. The first day of the rest of your life. Day one of your journey toward everything you've ever wanted; happiness, purpose, fulfillment, financial freedom, success, mental clarity, love, inner-discovery, and inner-peace. This is your time to design the life that you want for you; not for anyone else. This is for you.

The next thirty days of your life are centered around you and only you. Now, that might sound selfish to some of you reading this but, hey, guess what? It's the complete opposite.

You growing into the best version of yourself is beneficial for everyone surrounding you. I guarantee you that the better you feel about yourself; the better your relationships will become, the better your circumstances will become, and the better your overall quality of life will become.

Everything around you will begin to shift. The more you learn, the more you grow, the more you practice the skills that you will learn over the next thirty days, and the more you are in a positive mental and emotional state; the more you will start to see things change in your life. So, get ready to become the best "you" that there is and get ready to transform your life for the better. This is exactly what you're going to do over the next thirty days.

Thirty days from now, you can be in a completely new state emotionally, mentally, financially, spiritually, and physically. It's all up to you. You control your circumstances. You control your journey. Only you have the power to make this happen. No one else.

Beginning today, you can take control of your life. You can create your future. You can manifest your dreams into reality. You can make your own choices; even when you feel like that's not an option. This is your life and only you hold that power. No one else. Just you. Only you.

Forget what anyone else says. Forget what anyone else thinks. Forget about every single person who has ever doubted you or who has told you that you couldn't do something. Forget about all the negative things anyone has ever said about you. Fuck it. Forget it all. There's no room for that shit where you're headed.

You're headed to a place that is entirely consumed with your goals, your vision, your positivity, your values, your aspirations, your joys, your happiness, your peace, and your purpose. There's no room for doubt, negativity, hate, regret or other peoples' opinions where you're headed. Let that shit go. Out with the old, in with the new. Do it for you. Because let me tell you something: You need you more than you need them. Never forget that.

Let me say it again.
You need you more than you need them.

Let that sink in. Let it marinate for a minute. You need you more than you need them. These next thirty days are about you developing into the best version of you that there is. We're going to tap into everything that makes you "you." We're going to discover and bring out what makes you tick, what makes you inspired, what excites you, what motivates you, what sets your soul on fire, what makes you vulnerable, what challenges you, what has hurt you, and what has made you strong. We're going to face your fears, your doubts, your pain, your struggles, your heartache, your failures, and your greatest regrets. All of it. Every part.

This is it. It's your time. It's your turn. Here it is. You don't have to stress anymore. You don't have to search anymore. You don't have to hope that you had it better. You don't have to envy anyone else's life anymore. You don't have to want to be happier anymore. This is it right here in your hands: everything you need to know about this thing we call "life" and how to fucking take control of it and make it everything you've ever wanted.

Your journey awaits.

2

Un-do Your Past and Re-Create Your Future

"Your new life is going to cost you your old one."
– Unknown

There's an old saying by Umar bin al Kattab that goes a little something like this, *"Sometimes, people with the worst past create the best future."* I couldn't agree more.

Man. Just let that sink in. I strongly believe that everything in this life is by precise design. The pain, the suffering, the struggle, the regret, the heartache, and the losses. They all happened to prepare you for what's to come. These things don't define you. They served as lessons to direct you on a new path into the future.

Don't focus on them, don't obsess over them, don't regret them, don't be ashamed of them, and don't hold yourself back because of them. Recognize them, embrace them, learn from them, use them, and be grateful for them; for they shaped you into who you are today.

The direction you're heading toward in this life is much better than where you've been. This new version of your life is going to require a new and improved version of yourself. You're going to have to leave some things behind including other peoples' opinions, your doubts, your fears, your insecurities, your failures, and even some people who you once thought were friends. You must find the strength and the courage to leave those things behind so that you can make room for the new things that are coming to you.

Some things, situations, and people come into your life to teach you a lesson, open your eyes, direct you on a new path, or to heighten your sense of awareness. Let them but be wise enough and strong enough to let them go when it's time. Stop holding on to the past.

Everything in your life is happening for a reason whether it's positive or negative. One way or another, you attracted it into your life from previous thoughts, actions, or feelings.

If you're going through something negative right now and you want it to change; change your focus to something better and stick to it. If you're experiencing something positive and you want it to continue, then keep an attitude of gratitude. Embrace and enjoy the good things that are happening to you. With the right attitude, things will keep going good for you.

The bottom line is this: you attract things into your life based upon how you think and feel. Your thoughts impact your emotions. Your emotions impact your behavior. Your behavior impacts your actions. Your actions impact your consequences and, ultimately, your future; good or bad.

It all starts from one place: in your head. Think on that. Essentially, you can control your future if you just learn to control your thoughts. You hold the power to un-do your past and re-create your future.

That's your power.

3

Take Your Fucking Power Back

"You have the power within you to rise above
whatever is currently seeking to bring you down."
– Unknown

Today, I'm going to give you the cold, harsh truth. Some of it you might not want to read. You might want to put this book down or even throw it across the room by the time you're done reading today's chapter. But, guess what? I don't care.

Someone needs to tell you. Someone needed to tell me these things, but no one did. I had to learn them the hard way. So, here I am; telling you. So, toughen the fuck up and get ready to take your power back. Today. Not tomorrow. Not next week. Not next month. You need to start this shit today.

Enough sitting around and feeling sorry for yourself. Enough wishing and hoping that things will get better. Enough waiting around for things to happen. You know better than this. You know that you deserve better. You know that you're capable of achieving the things that you want to achieve in every area of your life. You know that action produces results. Productivity produces results. You already know this.

Get off your ass and go make something happen. Sitting there in your pathetic sorrows, waiting, and hoping for things to change is never going to work, but you already know that, don't you?

You want a change, then fucking change. Do something about it. Stop thinking about it. Stop hoping for it. Stop saying you'll start. Stop waiting for a better situation, circumstance, or sign to come along. Stop waiting on someone else to tell you to do it. Stop waiting on someone or something to validate it. You know the change you want; so, change. It's really that simple. Stop overthinking it. Stop trying to plan it all out before you begin. Just do it. Just start. That's it. Start today.

Don't forget everything you've learned over the years. Don't forget the pain you've endured to get here. You deserve this, and you owe it to yourself to not give up on yourself. Find ways to remind yourself of who you are. You did this. You survived everything to this day. You did that. You endured years of adversity to learn that you deserve better.

Every morning, you should remind yourself of this. I do. I set a reminder in my calendar every single morning. I read this chapter and other reminders to myself every morning at the same exact time. Most mornings, I honestly don't want to, but guess what? I do it anyway because I still want change. I still want to grow. I still want to develop. I still want to learn. I still want to succeed. I still have goals and milestones to accomplish. So, I remind myself every morning. It has and continues to make a significant impact in my life.

You know what you need to do. Do it for you. Start today. Take your fucking power back.

"Don't put off until tomorrow what you can do today."
— Benjamin Franklin

4

Strength in Pain

"What if everything you are going through is preparing you for what you asked for?"
– Unknown

"Strength isn't proven in the times where everything is going right in your life. Strength is proven in the times where everything is going wrong, but you gather the courage to smile, stay positive, keep it all together, trust the process, and move forward regardless."
– Elina Lee

You know the old saying, *"What doesn't kill you makes you stronger."* I'm here to tell you that after all I've personally been through, this statement couldn't be any truer. What doesn't kill you really does make you stronger. Your pain, struggle, and stress, while at the time may seem confusing, is all preparing, strengthening, and molding you into the person that you need to become. I know it might not seem that way in the moment but, trust me, there's a higher purpose for your pain. There is a lesson to be learned. There is a change to be made. It's all happening or has happened to you for a purpose.

Take it from someone who has endured struggle after struggle, survived abuse, overcame a juvenile criminal background, been told *"No"* a million times but still built the life and career I've always imagined having, and then lost it all. I've been there. I know what it feels like. I've also privately battled depression for the past decade. Almost every day of those years were painful, emotionally excruciating, mentally draining, and outright confusing.

I've cried myself to sleep countless nights. I've felt like there was no one else in the world who understood how much pain I was in. I've felt like there was no one else in the world who gave a damn. I've felt alone, broken, and helpless for years. I've had days where I couldn't bear to be in public because I was in so much pain on the inside. I've had my days where I had to make appearances, stand on stage, or produce events for clients and be sociable while I was screaming on the inside wanting to end my life. I've been there for many days for many years. I know what it's like.

For the past decade, I felt that I was living someone else's life at times. I lived a very public life with a man I didn't love and we both had very public careers that did not help to make matters better. I allowed myself to stay in an unhappy and unhealthy marriage while I privately dealt with depression, anxiety, emptiness, loneliness, and physical insecurity issues on my own. For years, I had to live my life pretending to be someone that I wasn't because of my marriage, my job title, and my reputation. I had to learn how to be strong for myself.

None of it was easy but it was all worth it. I found strength in my pain. I used it to become who I am today. It taught me to stand up for myself, to leave something that no longer served me, to build my own life, to find my own happiness, to have my own peace, and to design my own future.

At the time, I didn't know that life was preparing me to eventually lead, help, inspire, and coach others who also deal with depression, anxiety, and other struggles in their lives. I didn't know that I would eventually share my story with others and it would prevent them from committing suicide or that it would help to rekindle relationships with their family members that have been lost for years. I didn't know that my story would help to change the direction of so many other peoples' lives for the better. There was a purpose to my pain, but it was up to me to find the strength in myself to keep going.

Recognize your pain. Recognize your struggles. Understand and accept that, even though it hurts like hell right now, there is a purpose behind it. Everything that is happening to you or has happened to you is preparing you for who you need to be.

Even though, some days, it may seem confusing, remember that it's all by perfect design. Even though you may not be able to control the circumstances around you, you always have the power to control how you respond to them. That is your power.

Stay strong. You will get through this. You've survived everything else. You're a survivor. You're a fucking badass and you can have everything you want in life. So, hold your head up high and keep pushing forward. You got this.

"Everything will be okay in the end.
If it's not okay, it's not the end."
– John Lennon.

5

I'm Going to Make You So Proud - Note to Self

"You know who's going to give you everything? Yourself."
– Diane Von Furstenberg

Guess what? You're a badass. You're capable of so much more than you know. You really can have everything that you want in your life. You need to be reminded of it daily. Here's the sad part though: no one's going to remind you, so, you need to remind yourself. Every single day.

It's all up to you. You hold that power. No one else does and no one else ever will. Honestly, no one cares as much about your quality of life or your goals as you do. Why would you expect anyone else to do the work, care, and remind you that you're unstoppable and capable of achieving everything you desire? Why? Well, no one will. You must do that yourself. So, do it. Take that first step. Make a daily reminder to yourself and stick to it. Every single day.

You need to remind yourself what you want in life. What's your goal? What do you really want? Do you want to be happy? Do you want to be successful? Do you want financial freedom? Do you want to fall in love, get married, and have a happy family? Do you want that promotion at work? Do you want to travel the world? Do you want to move into that house? Do you want to be at peace every day? Do you want to live each day as stress-free as possible? Do you want more free time? Do you want stronger relationships with your loved ones? Do you want more friends? Do you want to be healthier? Do you want to get in shape?

What do you want? Write it down. Read it every day. No exceptions. Read it every single day and, as you read each item, visualize them in your mind. Imagine how you would feel if this happened. This is so important. Feel it. Imagine it's already happening and it's already a reality. How does that make you feel? Read and practice this every single day. Things will start to shift in your life. Effortlessly, naturally, rapidly. This is the first change you need to make to get on your path of achieving everything that you want in life.

Don't worry about the process of achieving what you want. Just focus on the end goal. Focus on how you will feel once it's yours. Everything else will work out along the way. Stop getting distracted by "how" you're going to achieve it. Just know that you eventually will, and it will be fucking awesome because that's what you deserve: fucking awesome. It's that simple. Practice this every single day.

Stop getting distracted by what other people have said about your goals. Do you really believe their opinion, or did someone just repeatedly tell you their opinion and you started to subconsciously believe them? That's probably the case. You know what you want. You know what you deserve. You know what you're good at. You know what kind of potential you have. No one else knows that better than you. So, take advantage of your potential. Use it before it's too late. Stop letting other people dictate how you should be living your life.

Don't stop until it's done. Don't rest until you're satisfied. You know what you need to do. Change. Just fucking do it. Don't let anyone tell you otherwise. Don't let anyone tell you you're dreaming too big, it's not worth it, it won't make you happy, or it won't make you successful. You know better. You know what's best for you. Don't listen to them. Do what's best for you and only you. You know exactly what you need to do. So, just do that.

Imagine if you would have started working toward what you wanted a year ago instead of beginning today. Where would you be today instead? Not where you're at right now. So, don't let that happen again. Don't wait another year or month or even a day to start to make a change. Take control starting today and make a difference in your own life and in your future.

You're a fucking badass. Start taking your own advice. Start living the life that you want to live. Start being the person that you want to be. One year from now, where do you want to be? Who do you want to be? Start being that person today. You're a fucking badass and you deserve it.

"I have specific goals. I don't have to explain myself any longer. After years of service to others, it's my turn to be selfish. I'm not sorry. I am optimistic and excited every day to wake up and accomplish another goal. You're allowed to terminate toxic relationships. You're allowed to walk away from people and situations that hurt you. You're allowed to be selfish. You don't owe anyone an explanation for taking care of yourself."
– Ciara Nichols

6

It's All by Design

"Anything that annoys you is teaching you patience. Anyone who abandons you is teaching you how to stand up on your own two feet. Anything that angers you is teaching you forgiveness and compassion. Anything that has power over you is teaching you how to take your power back. Anything you hate is teaching you unconditional love. Anything you fear is teaching you courage to overcome your fear. Anything you can't control is teaching you how to let go."
– Jackson Kiddard

I'm sure you've probably heard the saying, *'Everything happens for a reason."* about a million fucking times throughout your life. I know I have. Many people are skeptical and critical of this saying but I 100% stand by it.

I believe it's a matter of one's awareness and that there is a lesson to be learned in every life experience you have; you just need to be aware and observant enough to notice it. What you may have perceived to be a challenge, or a failure may have just been a setup for something bigger and better in your future.

Change can be painful, scary, hard, confusing, exciting, inspiring, and exhausting. Change can also make you feel like you're falling apart or make you regret the decisions that you made. You're not falling apart. You didn't make the wrong decision. You're just coming into something new and different with a new opportunity to make it bigger and better this time around. Sometimes, in life, everything must fall apart before it can be pieced back together.

You'll be amazed at how effortlessly and naturally things fall into place once you let go of trying to control everything, every situation, and every outcome around you. When you feel like you need to force something, or you need to use too much will power to make something happen, it's a sign that you should be doing the opposite. Sometimes, you need to just let go, trust the process, and go exactly where you're being led.

Not too long ago, I thought I had it all together. I was young, rich, successful, well-respected, and well-recognized in my industry. I was going places in life. I built a thriving multi-million-dollar company that allowed me to utilize my talents, make my own schedule, travel the world, experience new cultures, and inspire others to do the same. I just signed the papers to my very first home. It was my dream home (which, by the way, I completely and entirely attracted into my life using the Law of Attraction.)

It was an 8,400 square foot home on a lake and golf course in a coveted privately gated community in central Florida. Entirely custom built and designed, twelve seat state-of-the-art movie theater, four bars, three wine cellars, seven bathrooms, my own private office and library, personal gym, elevator, twenty-four-foot ceilings, beautiful columns and oversized windows throughout the home. It also had a $40,000 custom designed closet, private guest house, heated pool, heated marble floors (like who the fuck really needs heated floors in Florida?), sauna (and who the fuck really needs a sauna in Florida?), smart home system, everything you could ever want (or think you wanted….) in a home. It was a nice fucking house; the nicest house I've ever stepped foot into in my entire life. That's still true to this day.

My life seemed great. I was the woman who had it all together. Other women looked up to me and wanted to be me. I always thought to myself, "Why? I get it. I'm rich. I'm successful but I don't have my shit together. I'm a fucking mess. I have money, yes. Sure, but everything else in my life fucking sucks. I'm depressed. I'm angry. I'm sad. I'm lonely. I have no friends. I've never been in love. I'm forced to stay married to a man and business partner I despise to keep all of these 'things.' Being successful and working hard is an escape for me. That's how I got rich. I poured myself into my work to escape reality. But guess what? It fucking sucks. I would never want this quality of life for anyone."

I spent so many years of my life believing what so many others believe: Money buys happiness. So, I worked hard for almost a decade to make as much money as I could. I wanted to become successful. I wanted to become rich. I slaved my twenties away. I sacrificed my friendships. I sacrificed my relationships. I sacrificed my time. I sacrificed my sanity. I sacrificed my hobbies. I sacrificed every part of me that made me "me" until work just became my life because that was all I knew.

Now, there is a healthy way to do this. Don't get me wrong: sacrificing for what you want to achieve is a good thing (a great fucking thing and everyone should do it); if and only if it's implemented correctly. My approach to this concept was entirely wrong and I'm not ashamed to admit that. I fucked up. I fucked up big time.

I was twenty years old when I started my first company and I started it with the intentions of "getting rich." It worked but, when I was rich, I realized that a larger part of me was missing. "I" was missing. I spent all these years working to get rich that I lost myself. I forgot who I was. I forgot what made me happy. I forgot how to have friends. I forgot how to have relationships. I forgot how to enjoy life. I forgot how to be myself. I forgot how to "live."

By all means; sacrifice your time and effort for what you believe in and for what you want to accomplish in life. Please. Just don't do what I did. Don't become so entirely obsessed and focused on becoming "successful" and "rich" that you forget to live your life, develop yourself as a person, and enjoy your loved ones.

Success is all about balance. You really can have it all. There's no point in making millions if you have no one to share it with. There's no point in living in a mansion if it's not a happy home. Money will not buy you happiness. Trust me. I was successful but still suffered from severe depression, anxiety, and constant thoughts of suicide.

Some of the happiest moments that I had in life occurred before my success; when money was the last thing on my mind. Those moments happened when I was spending time with my loved ones, working on my personal development, and doing the things that I loved. I was broke, grateful, loved, and happy. Money had nothing to do with my happiness before success and money has nothing to do with my happiness now either.

I spent most of the past decade wanting to leave and start over, but I never could. I honestly could never find the courage or the strength within myself to just take the jump. I always considered myself a risk taker, so, not being able to do the one thing that I wanted to do made me feel insecure in myself. It made me feel less of a person. It made me feel that maybe I wasn't as strong or as brave as I thought I was.

This type of behavior, insecurity, and negative-self talk only pushed me farther and farther into depression. I was digging my own hole and the hole just kept getting deeper and deeper over the years.

It also didn't help that my husband/business partner at the time only seemed to be focused on the business, as well. He never showed much interest in me as a person and when I did try to open up to him about my depression, he made me feel wrong for the emotions that I was experiencing. He made me feel ashamed and embarrassed for being diagnosed with depression, so, I just spent the next several years hiding it from the rest of the world, too, because he made me believe they would feel the same. I started to believe that they would think I was insane, weak, mentally unstable, and that I wasn't fit to run a company. So, I put my emotions in a box and didn't open the box until eight years later.

That's when everything in my life started to shift. Things suddenly started to make sense. I started to understand why I was feeling the way I felt each day. The pain, anger, resentment, regret, and suffering all started to make sense.

I wasn't happy. I knew something had to change and, deep down, I always knew that I would have to leave everything behind for that to happen. It was always a thought in the back of my mind for years. It was as if my subconscious or maybe even a higher power beyond myself was trying to tell me something, but I ignored it for years.

So, that's exactly what I did. I finally had enough. I left it all behind. It was the hardest decision I have ever made in my life, but I knew it was what had to be done. Everything changed. I no longer was rich. I no longer lived in a mansion. I no longer drove a Mercedes GL450. I no longer was able to travel the world at will.

But, more importantly, I no longer lived every day in a dark and lonely depression. I no longer cried myself to sleep at night. I no longer woke up not wanting to live. I no longer felt alone. I no longer felt empty inside. I no longer was in pain. I no longer bruised, cut, or damaged my hands from punching bags trying to release my anger and frustration. I no longer had to sit in my office for twelve hours doing something I didn't enjoy or believe in. I no longer had to put on a facade for people. I no longer cared about anyone else's opinion.

I was free. Free from everything that held me back for almost a decade. Just like that. One decision. One action. One choice changed the entire course and direction of my life and future. Just like that. It was all by design. Everything that had happened over the years that I thought was a failure or a struggle was all leading me up to this very moment. It all made sense. So, I trusted it and, just like that, everything changed.

Life has a funny way of teaching us things. In the moment, you may feel like everything is falling apart around you, it's all just coming together. Change is necessary for growth. Trust the process and remind yourself that everything is happening in perfect timing and by perfect design. It all serves a purpose. There is a learning lesson in every life experience. You just need to be aware and observant enough to notice it.

7

Vulnerability is Strength

"To share your weakness is to make yourself vulnerable; to make yourself vulnerable is to show your strength."
– Criss Jami

I get it. It's uncomfortable to open up to people. We've all had struggles with it at one time or another in our lives. It's instinctual to avoid situations and conversations that feel uncomfortable or may pose a threat to us getting "hurt" emotionally. This is completely normal. You're not the only one who deals with this. We all do. Most of us will just never admit it.

Our brains are wired to protect us which is why many of us resort to keeping our feelings to ourselves, not sharing our fears, not talking about our struggles, not telling someone what they mean to us, and so on. We fear what others may think. We don't want them to think we're being weak, sensitive, overly-emotional, or too touchy-feely. We overthink it and we eventually fall into the trap that we set for ourselves through our own hypothetical and pre-determined scenarios and lies that we build up in our minds of how someone will respond if we "open up." This type of thinking will never get us anywhere.

Here's the cold, hard truth: If you ever want to have a meaningful relationship with another human being or with yourself, then vulnerability is a requirement. It's not an option. It is absolutely a requirement. Stop lying to yourself.

Like I said, I get it. I've been there. I've always lived my life under the assumption that I had to be "strong." For years, I tried to conceal my depression, pain, sadness, insecurities, and anxiety because I was taught that these emotions were a sign of weakness. I was so wrong. Real strength is found when you can get in touch with your emotions, be vulnerable, and gather the courage that it takes to express them openly and honestly with other people. That's strength. It wasn't until I completely opened up about my depression, anxiety, and past experiences during this past year that I finally felt "strong" and empowered.

Finally being able to openly share this story with someone was one of the hardest conversations that I've ever had in my life. I had kept this story in the very back of my mind for so many years; subconsciously hoping that maybe I would just forget about it. That obviously didn't happen. It only caused me more pain and other issues over the years. I was ashamed that it happened to me. I was angered by it. I was frustrated by it. I was disgusted by it. I even blamed myself for it happening even though I knew it wasn't my fault and it was out of my control.

I've had a painful list of "what ifs" run through my mind so many times. I kept all these emotions locked away inside of me for so many years. They just built up and festered. I couldn't gather the courage to even speak about this story, so, an old friend found the courage for me. He helped me find the strength to talk about it. He made me comfortable enough to share it with him. He allowed me to be vulnerable with him. He made me understand that I was in a safe place; and when I was able to be vulnerable, I had never felt stronger.

I remember sitting there with him wanting to tell him everything and the words just wouldn't come out of my mouth. My chest was tight, eyes watering, anger rising, and heartbeat accelerating. Then I would go to speak and nothing. I would try to gather the strength to say the first few words….and nothing. We just sat there in silence. A painful silence. And, then, it was like time stopped. Everything stopped. All the emotions came rushing back immediately. It was intense. It was painful. I started to picture it happening in my mind. I could see it all again. Everything that I've tried to erase from my memory all came rushing back in seconds. And, then, I was numb. So, I spoke. And I shared. And I cried. And I hurt.

When I finished talking, I literally felt like a new person. After sharing this story and many other stories with my friend, I realized that much of this was why I've been dealing with depression and anxiety for the past decade. I never allowed myself to confront what happened to me. I tried to force myself to forget about it and so many other things from my past. I tried to distract myself with work. I tried to ignore and erase my emotions. None of these things worked. They only made it worse.

So, by now, I'm sure you're probably thinking to yourself, "What the fuck happened?" Well, now that I've finally found the strength to share this story out loud, I want to share it with you, too. Maybe you or someone you know has experienced something similar. Maybe this story will help you or them find strength in vulnerability, too.

So, here goes nothing: I was twenty years old and had just started a new job at a marketing firm. I left home several months earlier to move to the big city, try life out on my own, be a "grown-up," finish my bachelor's degree, and pursue my doctorate's degree in Physical Therapy. I thought I had it all figured out.

All of my bills were paid on time, I had my own two-bedroom apartment in a great area, a new car, my two-year-old son was enrolled in a great daycare, I had a great support system of friends, I was an honorary sorority member, I was on the dean's list, I maintained a 4.0 GPA for most of my collegiate career, I had my future mapped out, and even knew where I wanted to complete my physical therapy residency down the road.

Then it happened, and everything fell apart. It was a series of unfortunate events. One thing after another. I had to leave my job, I was running out of money, I couldn't focus in class, my grades were falling, I was distracted, I was angry, I was scared, I resorted to drinking and partying to try to numb the pain, and I had to move because someone tried to break into my apartment (I remember sitting at my kitchen table late one night studying and I sneezed. I heard someone say, "Bless you." So, I looked up and there was someone standing inside my porch by the living room glass door, staring at me. I could hear noises that night. The noises turned out to be a man cutting the screen and moving my outdoor furniture, so he could make his way to the glass door to watch me. Both of his hands and face were imprinted on the glass. The police couldn't do anything about it the next morning. I didn't feel safe, so, I left.).

I didn't have anywhere to go. My parents were going through a divorce at the time. My brother was living with his friends at a bachelor pad. I couldn't take my son there. I eventually ended up moving in with a friend who I would later build my first business with, marry, divorce, and leave him with everything. I never allowed myself the time to cope or heal after what happened. Everything in my life seemed to keep falling out of my control to where I ended up in an unhealthy marriage and situation for the next several years. The only thing that made me feel in control and stable was work. So, I built a company, made a lot of money, became very successful very fast, and years later, realized that I was still depressed and had never healed.

At my marketing job, I had the opportunity to travel across Louisiana, Mississippi, Alabama, and Florida. The firm provided me with a company car, hotel rooms, and company money for my expenses. I also made a decent amount of money for having no degree and no prior experience. Everyone at the firm seemed great. They all seemed to be very family oriented, professional, and nice. I thought this would be a great place for me to learn new skills and make a decent living while I finished my degrees. And, I guess it would have been.... Maybe, if I were a man but, that wasn't the case here.

There was a company retreat planned at a cabin a few hours away that would take place over the weekend. We all traveled often so this seemed like a great idea for us to slow down, get a break, and enjoy life. My boss was so excited about it. He told me that everyone at the firm was coming. He said that we were going to celebrate, sit around the fire, talk business, discuss new ideas and concepts for the future, get to know everyone at the firm, enjoy the great outdoors, and just relax. I was excited. I loved cabins, I loved the country, I loved being outside, I loved campfires, I loved meeting new people, and I loved talking business and the future.

All of it sounded so great. So, I drove over six hours to the address that he gave me under the impression that everyone at the firm was going to be there for the company retreat. I listened to my GPS, turned down a country road, and then onto a long, un-marked gravel driveway that eventually led to a secluded cabin on a river. There were only two other cars there. Something didn't feel right. This cabin was in the middle of nowhere. There was nothing around us but woods and a river. No neighbors. Nothing. Something wasn't right.

I parked, took my suit case out of my car, and greeted him. Everything seemed normal. He was there with one other man that I've met before who also worked at the firm. They were acting just fine; nothing out of the ordinary. Maybe everything really was fine, and I was just overthinking like usual. I waited for hours for the others to show up and it didn't happen. They said everyone was running "late as usual." So, while we waited, we ate dinner, had a couple drinks, and started talking about work. Then, two other men showed up. One who supposedly helped start the firm and the other was a business associate of theirs.

At this point, I'm feeling entirely uncomfortable being the only woman in a cabin full of strange men. I tried texting and calling my boyfriend at the time to tell him that I didn't feel comfortable being there. Just my luck; no service. My phone didn't work. So, here I was in the middle of nowhere, without a phone, alone in a cabin with a handful of men that I didn't really know in a foreign town that I've never been to or heard of. Great.

It gets later. Everyone is standing outside by the fire, so, I decide to join them. Everyone is still acting normal, they're all talking business, discussing old clients, new clients, old deals, and new deals. Then, one of them brings out this bottle of tequila that they bought in Mexico. I remember it so vividly because there was a worm floating around in the bottle. We all took a shot to celebrate the future and, after that, I decided it was time for me to go to my room and rest. I remember when I told everyone that I was heading in for the night, my boss looked at me in an obscure way; a way I've never seen before. I didn't like it. Something wasn't right.

He followed me as I walked backed into the cabin and was acting very strange like he didn't want me to leave. I told him, "Good night," and I went upstairs into the room they had set aside for me. I had another bad feeling. Something wasn't right. My room was at the top of the stairs. It reminded me of an attic. I can still see every part of it in detail. It was dark, large, and empty with only a small, old-fashioned, wooden, country-style bed in the middle of the room with a lightly colored quilt covering it, and two pillows. The ceiling was low, diagonal, and pointed where it met in the middle of the room. I remember staring at the crease in the ceiling later that night unable to move.

There was a small bathroom down the hall. After I finished getting dressed and ready in the bathroom, I went back into my room to go to sleep. I closed the door behind me and went to lock the door. There wasn't a lock. I didn't like this. Something wasn't right. I was starting to feel disoriented, exhausted, and nauseous. All I wanted to do was sleep, wake up, and leave first thing in the morning.

Later that night, I heard a noise. I woke up and saw a light from the hall. The door was opening, and someone was coming in. I was so tired and disoriented that I couldn't tell if I was awake or if I was still sleeping. Then, he came into my bed and had his way with me. I remember knowing what was happening but not feeling in control of the moment or myself. I could see everything, feel everything, taste everything. I remember him shoving his tongue into my mouth and making me do things to him. I wanted it to stop. I wanted to vomit. I wanted to cry. I wanted to disappear. I wanted to die but I couldn't do any of these things. I just became numb. I eventually felt nothing. No pain. No emotion. No anger. No sadness. Nothing. Numb.

I left the next morning. Confused, scared, disgusted, angry, helpless, frustrated, and alone. I wasn't all there. I couldn't think clearly. Did this just happen to me? Then everything just went away, and I was numb again, and I stayed numb for the next several years. I never told anyone until I told my friend eight years after it happened and, now, I'm telling you.

"Owning our story can be hard but not nearly as difficult as spending our lives running from it. Embracing our vulnerabilities is risky but not nearly as dangerous as giving up. Only when we are brave enough to explore the darkness will we discover the infinite power of our light."
— Brene Brown

8

Don't Sweat the Small Shit

"The only thing that makes it a part of your life
is that you keep thinking about it."
– Unknown

During the past year, I've started this new thing where I trained myself mentally to not "sweat the small shit." Trust me; this is easier said than done, especially when you suffer from severe anxiety like I do.

Even though I've been practicing this theory for a year, I still have my days where I fall into my self-destructive thoughts. My anxiety will kick in and I'll feel like I'm losing control. It will feel like a hundred thoughts are running through my mind at any given moment. It's impossible to focus. I'll start to overanalyze and pick apart everything and every person around me. I'll start to question my feelings, emotions, and decisions. I'll subconsciously start to build an endless list of "what-if's" in my mind. I'll feel angry then happy then sad then numb then frustrated, all in a matter of minutes. Some days, my mind gets the best of me and I feel like I have no control over it. But, then, I catch myself and I remind myself that I, in fact, do have control. This is my mind. I am the master of it; it is not the master of me. Despite how entirely frustrating and exhausting anxiety and overthinking is, there are ways to overcome it, learn from it, and grow even stronger and more aware than you were before.

When I recognize that my anxiety is kicking back in, I make myself find a quiet place where I can be alone with my thoughts. I close my eyes, breath in, and breath out to pull myself out of this self-destructive cycle of anxiety and over-thinking. Deep breaths. Then, I speak to myself internally. You can also speak to yourself out loud; do what works for you.

Positive self-talk is so crucial in the beginning of this process. I tell myself, "Relax, Elina. Just let it go. Stop overanalyzing. Stop overthinking. Stop stressing. Stop worrying. Just relax. Let it all go. Stop thinking. Start feeling." And, then, I silence my mind. No verbal thoughts. No more talking to myself. No more thinking about what I want to eat later. No more thinking about what I forgot to do yesterday. No more thinking about anything. Complete silence; internally and externally. And, as soon as a thought tries to slide in there, I immediately stop it and continue focusing on the silence and my breathing. Try this practice for a few minutes the next time you catch yourself overthinking, feeling anxious, stressing about something, or if you just want to feel relaxed, aware, in tune, and present.

1. Find a quiet place.

2. Lay down. Legs together. Back straight. Arms by your side or stretched above your head. (You can also do this practice in a seated position, but I find that I relax more while I'm laying down.)

3. Close your eyes.

4. Relax.

5. Deep breath in through your nostrils.
   Fill your lungs with as much air as you can with each breath. (I usually start by slowly counting to five as I inhale, hold, and let the breath roll into an exhale; slowly counting to five as I exhale.)

6. Exhale slowly through your mouth.

7. Continue this deep breathing cycle throughout the practice.

8. Relax.

9. Positive Self-Talk. You can speak this out loud or you can speak it internally. Tell yourself, "Relax. Just let it go. Stop overanalyzing. Stop overthinking. Stop stressing. Stop worrying. Just relax. Let it all go. Stop thinking. Start feeling. Let it go."

10. Relax.

11. Silence your mind. No more thoughts. As soon as a thought comes, recognize it and immediately end it by continuing to focus on the silence and your breathing.

Try this for a few minutes or even longer. Do it for as long or as short as you need to. If you do it right, you'll come out of this practice feeling like a brand-new person. When your mind is clear, you're able to perform better in all areas of life. Overthinking and overanalyzing cloud your vision and judgement; they cloud your capabilities to become the best version of yourself and, sometimes, prevent you from completing simple day-to-day tasks efficiently.

When you have a clear mind, you'll have more awareness. You'll begin to have more of a sense of who you are and what you enjoy. You'll feel inspired. You'll feel positive. You'll feel happy. You'll feel at ease. Things that used to bother you and occupy your mind no longer will. You will begin to attract better circumstances into your life.

Practice this often. Doing it once or twice won't make a significant difference in your life. It will make a difference immediately, but it won't last. Therefore, it is so crucial that you make this a practice; make it a habit. Do it as often as you can. Stop thinking. Start feeling. Let it go. Let it all go.

9

You'll Never Know What You're Capable of Until You Try

"Strength doesn't come from what you can do. It comes from overcoming the things you once thought you couldn't."
– Rikki Rogers

Every now and then, we all need to be reminded of what we're capable of. The ugly truth behind that concept, though, is that you can't really depend on other people to do that for you. It just doesn't work that way. You must remind yourself. Never allow someone's negative limitations to keep you from believing in yourself or your dreams. Their doubt reflects their limitations; not yours. Don't give up on yourself. Ever.

Remind yourself of just how strong you are. You are talented. You are worth it. You have a purpose. You have the potential to accomplish everything in life that you want. You deserve to happy. You deserve to be successful. You deserve love. You deserve excitement. You deserve peace. You deserve adventure. You deserve abundance. You deserve to grow into all that you can be. Everything that you want, guess what? You deserve it. You can have it all.

But, it's going to take some work. You can't just snap your fingers and expect to be happy and successful overnight. It's a process. It's an acquired skill. It takes practice. It takes patience. But, guess what? You're capable and you deserve to live the life that you desire. You deserve to have everything you ever set your mind, eyes, and intentions on. It's yours. You deserve it. Own it.

As humans, we have the capabilities to adapt, evolve, and learn new skills. We're unlike any other being in the world. We have the power to mold and shape our environment, our opinions, and our future. We should all take advantage of that.

We should become addicted to enhancing ourselves in every single area of our lives. There is no limit as to how far the mind can go. Enhance it. Teach it. Strengthen in. Feed it. Learn a new skill. Learn a new language. Practice and perfect a talent.

What good is your potential if you're not utilizing it? You can choose to develop your mental resources, or you can just waste them away. The choice is ultimately yours.

Take advantage of the fact and opportunity that you have control of your reaction to every circumstance, situation, and environment. You may not be able to control everything happening around you, but you can always control of your response to them.

"*Until you spread your wings, you'll*
never know how far *you can fly.*"
– *Unknown*

10

Your Vibe Attracts Your Tribe

"When you associate with winners,
your chances of winning go up."
– Zig Ziglar

It's an old saying that never gets old: *"The better you become, the better you attract."*

The universe likes speed. When you have a sense of who you are as a person or a sense of what your vision is to accomplish, the universe will do this thing where it aligns you with others on the same path and mission. Pay close attention to the circumstances and signs around you. When you have that "feeling" that someone came into your life for a reason; you're probably 100% right. Trust it. Embrace it. Appreciate it and take full fucking advantage of it.

Some opportunities only present themselves once. If you meet someone, whether it's regarding business, friendships, relationships, etc., and you have that "feeling;" you better act on it. Ten times out of ten, that person came into your life for a reason. You crossed paths for a purpose. If you don't act on your intuition, you could miss out on that opportunity that could lead to changing everything.

Honestly, you never know what could happen. One person could come along and change the entire course of your life for the better. You never know who or when that could happen. So, always go with your gut instinct and act when you feel an intuitive push to act.

It's inevitable: your environment shapes you. You become like the people you surround yourself with. So, choose wisely. Surround yourself with people who encourage you, motivate you, push you, and challenge you to be better. Friends want to see friends succeed and they celebrate one another's success.

It is so necessary to surround yourself with people who feed your energy. If they drain your energy, you have some reconsidering to do in your personal relationships. If you have someone in your life who drains your energy and doesn't support your dreams and aspirations, let them go. Bye, Felicia.

It's not your job to make others feel happy or positive. And, trust me, you will absolutely drain your own energy and lose your own motivation while trying to keep someone else's energy up. Don't sacrifice your mental well-being for another; ever. Get rid of the energy drainers. Get rid of the negative nay-sayers in your life. Get rid of the people who put you in a bad mood; the people who always seem to be in a bad mood.

The worst type of people are those who see that you're in a good mood and will do everything in their power to change that; the people who try to get you to lower yourself to their level are the exact type of people you need to avoid and get out of your life. These people are toxic and will only hinder your growth.

Positive vibes only.

When you find mutual empowerment with others on the same mission, something incredibly beautiful happens. Instead of viewing others as your competition, learn to encourage one another, and feed off each other's positive energy; whether it's your friend, a colleague, a stranger, or even someone you see on social media. Grow together. Learn together. Conquer together. Build together. Encourage each other. It's hard enough for people in society today to feel happy, strong, confident, and successful. Let's stop tearing each other down and begin lifting each other up. We should all be trying to win together.

"May you attract someone who
can keep up with you goal wise"
– Lalah Delia

11

Your Circumstances Do Not Define You

"What defines you as a person is not the life
you were born in to, but what you made of it."
– Shahid Kapoor

I'll never forget the moment I realized that I "discovered" myself. For years, I always thought I was trying to discover myself until I suddenly realized that I had done this years ago.

I hit hard times after achieving the largest amount of success and earning the largest amount of money that I had earned to this day. This was all self-inflicted and by choice, but it still had a detrimental and emotional impact on me. I went from living in an 8,400 square foot home to sharing the spare bedroom at my dad's house with my ten-year-old son. I went from being able to afford anything I wanted to be having to ask my family to borrow money and having to use food stamps to be able to feed myself and my son for several months while I re-built my life.

Life was different; different but necessary. I needed this to happen to me. I needed to be humbled. I needed to be brought back down to earth. I needed to struggle again. I needed to be reminded of what was really of importance in life: it wasn't success, it wasn't riches; it was family, support, and love. My eyes were opening. My ears were listening. The universe was trying to teach me a lesson.

During this time, Jason, a business colleague and good friend said to me, "You know what I admire about you? You never change. You are always constant. No matter how good things are or how bad things have been over the years, who you are never changes." Then it hit me. He was right.

How has this concept never crossed my mind before? He was so right. Throughout my entire life, especially in business, I never stopped believing in myself. I have always been confident in who I was as a person. I have always believed in myself; especially in the hard times. If anything, I believed in myself more during the hard times. Who I was never changed because of my environment or my circumstances.

I still had the same amount of confidence when I was twenty years old living on a mattress behind someone's couch staying up until three in the morning building a company on a broken laptop as I did when I was twenty-seven years old living in an 8,400 square foot home staying up until three in the morning in my executive office expanding multiple companies working on a top of the line computer.

Who I was never changed based on the situation I was in. I walked away from that life because it no longer served me internally and I set out on a new path toward fulfillment; the path that led me to write this book that you're holding in your hands right now. I left my wealth and success to live in the spare bedroom of my dad's house when I was twenty-eight years old. Who I was still didn't change. I still believed in myself even though my entire world had been turned upside down and everything I knew was gone.

My lifestyle was gone. My world travels were gone. My office and team of employees were gone. My home was gone. My money was gone but you know what never left and never changed? My soul, my core, my heart, my passion, my purpose, and my strength. If anything, those things only grew stronger and more solid when I was faced with adversity and struggle.

Who I was as a person never changed. I didn't lose myself because I lost everything around me. "Things" don't make a person. Your core, your beliefs, your values, your drive, and your happiness; that's what makes you. If you're aware of what those are then they will always be constant. They will never change because your life became a little uncomfortable. They will never change because you lost your job, or your bank account is in the negative. They will never change if the love of your life walked out on you.

When you have sense of who you are and where your values lie, nothing should ever fucking change that. That's who you are. Who you are is not defined by the amount of money you have, the relationship you're in, the amount of success you achieve, the type of house you live in, or what car you drive. Those are all superficial things. What really matters is what's internal. That's who you are and that should never change based on your circumstances.

12

You Create Your Reality: How to Use the Law of Attraction to Change Your Life

"The Law of Attraction: When you truly want something and go after it without limiting yourself with disbelief, the Universe will make it happen."
– Unknown

Summed up, the Law of Attraction states that what you can conceive in your mind, you can eventually turn into reality with the proper amount of energy and focus invested into manifesting it. Basically, whatever you imagine, you can create.

I've personally studied and practiced the Law of Attraction over the past decade and owe all my success to it. When I was twenty years old, I was introduced to the film, "The Secret." If you haven't seen it yet, I highly recommend watching it. If you have seen it, I highly recommend watching it as often as possible. It's on Netflix and YouTube. You have no excuse to not watch it.

I've probably watched and listened to "The Secret" several thousand times by now. Each time, I learn something new. I have an audio file of it on my phone so, some days, when I'm in the office, driving, or exercising, I'll play it repeatedly in the background. I fall asleep to it most nights, so, my brain is still subconsciously soaking it all in. This film and this law literally consumed and changed my life. I couldn't be more grateful and excited for it.

There are many ways you can begin to implement and incorporate the Law of Attraction into your life. You can start by writing a list of the things that you want to accomplish. You can create a vision board. You can have conversations with others. You can meditate, or you can just simply focus on what you want to attract into your life. There are so many ways to begin practicing the Law of Attraction. Whatever it is that you want to achieve in your personal life; write it down, set it as your computer screen or the background on your phone, write it on a post-it-note and stick it somewhere you will see it often, whatever works best for you; do that.

Then, once you've done that, envision being that future version of yourself and accomplishing those goals. Feel it. Imagine it. Pour your passion into it. The more energy and passion you put into what you want, the faster it will come to you. You must feel it. You can't just think about it. You can't just create an idea of it in your mind. You absolutely 100% must feel it and believe it. Imagine and pretend you already have it. Imagine how you'll feel when you do accomplish what it is that you're seeking.

Let's try it. Seriously. Right now, put this book down and take a couple minutes to do this. Go to a quiet place away from the distractions and noise, even if that means locking the bathroom door and hiding in there for a few moments (Honestly, I used to have to do this all the time. It was the only place I could get some peace and quiet. No shame.)

Wherever you need to go to have privacy, go there. Right now. Take a moment to yourself. Close your eyes. You know what it is that you want for your life regardless of the story that you tell yourself. Deep down, you know what you want. Envision that. Now, imagine yourself having that; whatever it may be.

How does it feel?

It feels pretty fucking good, doesn't it? You feel happy. You feel accomplished. You feel empowered. You feel proud. You feel free. You feel confident. You feel strong. You feel like you deserve this because……guess what? You do. You deserve all of this and so much more. This is just the first part of everything great that you will receive into your life. You deserve this. You deserve to feel this good all the time.

The more you are in this state of gratitude, passion, and empowerment; the more greatness you will attract into your life and into your world. The more you are in this state; the faster it will become your reality.

You might be asking yourself, "How can I feel grateful for something I don't even have?" Well, your mind is a very powerful tool. Your energy is even more powerful. With these two combined, you can create any reality that you desire. You can still feel grateful for people, things, or situations that aren't currently present in your life today. That's the secret to it all. You must envision yourself having that; already having, accomplishing, and enjoying what it is that you're seeking.

Feel it. Feel it as if it's right there in your life right now; today. Now, believe that you deserve it. Accept it, embrace it, receive it. Now, watch as it starts to make its way toward you. Practice this as often as possible. Doing it once won't make a significant difference in your life. This is something that must be repeated and practiced multiple times for it to be effective.

You create your reality. Only you.

13

Merry Christmas

"If you can imagine it in your mind,
you can experience it in your reality."
– Unknown

The Law of Attraction truly is an incredible thing. Since I was eighteen years old, I have been practicing, studying, and implementing the Law of Attraction into my life on a regular basis. It's been quite a journey……and not an easy one.

Some days, I wanted to quit and give it all up. Some days, I wanted to disappear from everyone and everything. Even on those days, I forced myself to change my mindset and would remind myself of just how powerful my mind and energy are and how impactful these negative thoughts and feelings would play a part in my days to come.

Practicing the Law of Attraction is how I was able to become successful in business, get in the best shape of my life, become a millionaire by the age of twenty-four, travel to numerous countries, experience the finer things in life, and so on. More importantly, it was how I eventually achieved my goal of becoming happy, experiencing true freedom, living my passions, falling in love, and starting a family, business and a life that I loved.

So, let me tell you a quick little story on one of my recent experiences with the Law of Attraction to put it all into perspective for you. Do you ever have those moments where you can't tell if you're awake or if you're dreaming; what's real and what's not? Well, this was one of those moments for me.

Last year, I gave myself a present on Christmas Eve. I didn't tell anyone about it; it was just something that I did for myself. I wrote a letter addressed to myself, from myself. I wrote the letter as if I were a future version of myself a year later. I promised myself that I would read it on Christmas morning of the next year and that everything in my letter would have come true. Sounds insane, doesn't it?

Well, a couple months later, I happened to come across this letter at random in my Samsung Notes App. I completely forgot that I even wrote it. It was mixed in with my other writing but, for some reason, it caught my attention and drew me in. So, I began reading it and everything around me stopped. I couldn't believe it. Everything in my letter had already manifested and became my reality. Every. Single. Thing.

Here's what my letter said:

December 24, 2017

"I'm so glad that I finally gathered enough courage to leave everything negative behind. It was the most terrifying decision that I ever made but I'm so glad that I finally made it. I left everything that didn't make me happy and everything that made me feel trapped or held me back from my potential.

Now, I'm free. I'm at peace and, every day, I'm living my dream by becoming a better version of myself. I'm able to spend my days doing what I love and being around those I care about the most; my family. I'm able to do the things I wasn't able to do in my controlling relationship before: like be myself, imagine, read, write, challenge myself, travel with my family, have friends and a social life, meditate, go on adventures by myself, take pictures without someone making me feel insecure or uncomfortable, make inspirational videos, build a business of my own, but most importantly, experience inner-peace and self-love every day.

I've become involved in multiple charities and I'm able to regularly donate my time to trying to make the world a better place. I've also started my own business that helps people around the world. Countless people are inspired by my story, life lessons, and prior hardships.

I've learned that everything negative that has happened to me has shaped and molded me to this very moment. It's given me the strength and the courage to share what I've learned with other people in order to help them in their daily lives.

I've learned so much since I left. Everything is different. My mind is free. I'm no longer a prisoner in a life that I allowed someone else to influence and shape for me for so many years. I have confidence in myself and in my dreams now. I believe anything is possible. I feel joy all the time. I've built incredible friendships; something I couldn't do for almost ten years. I've traveled and experienced different cultures. I've grown closer to my family. I don't wake up every day pissed off at the world and disgusted by the person I was in a relationship with. I don't feel clenched up inside anymore.

It's mind-blowing what can happen when you eliminate everything negative in your life. You become free. You see the world in a different light. It's beautiful."

I wrote this on Christmas Eve and, since that night, everything in my letter naturally and effortlessly started piecing together. I didn't even know it was happening. Everything that I envisioned came true and is continuing to build into something even greater every day.

Merry Christmas.
Anything is possible.

14

Self-Love is the Best Love

"Work on being in love with the person in the mirror who has been through so much but is still standing."
– Unknown

Today, I want you to do something. I want you to go stand in front of a mirror and just stare at yourself. Examine yourself. Study yourself. Inward and outward. Become as aware of yourself as you can in this very moment. I want you to become as extrinsically and intrinsically aware of who you are and what it is that you want in this life. I want you to venture and explore yourself inside out.

Who are you, really? Do you like what you see, or do you see something less desirable? Is the person staring back at you who you imagined yourself becoming a year ago? Five years ago? Ten years ago? Do you appreciate who you are? Do you admire all that you have accomplished? Whether you answered, "Yes" or "No," you are right.

Now, I'm going to teach you something today that society won't: *When you look at yourself in the mirror, you should love everything about you.* We're not just talking looks here. We're talking mind, body, *and* soul. You should have an intense and insatiable love for yourself. Now, as humans, we're naturally drawn to find faults in ourselves. This is ok. This is normal. I didn't say you had to like everything about yourself. I said you should love everything about yourself. The things you don't like, you have the power to change. That's the beauty of it. We're human. We have the capability to grow, enhance, learn, change, adapt, and evolve at will.

What you don't like is a product of your past actions and reactions. You don't like the extra weight you're carrying around? Practice a healthier lifestyle and adopt a healthier diet. You don't like how you often feel sad? Practice gratitude. You don't like that you're lonely? Take your sorry ass somewhere and meet new people or call an old friend. No one is ever truly alone. There are over seven billion humans in this world, I'm sure at least one of us will be there for you in your time of need. You can't get motivated? Remember what excites you and what makes you feel alive. What you don't like, you have the power to change.

What you should love, however, is you're the only person who will ever stare back at you when you look in that mirror. To this day, nothing has held you back or destroyed you because you're standing here looking at yourself right now. You are uniquely crafted to be exactly who you are just the way you are. You are capable of so much more than you give yourself credit for. You matter. You have a purpose. You are strong. You are enough. You are worth it. You continue to grow. You continue to learn. You continue to move forward regardless of anything that has ever tried to hold you back. You are a warrior. You are a survivor.

You are different from everyone else and you know that. You deserve to be happy. You deserve to live a life of abundance. You deserve to experience your passions. You deserve to live a life you're excited about. You should fucking love yourself. You deserve it and you owe it to yourself. Don't ever doubt your worth. Stop underestimating yourself. Own who you are. Appreciate who you are. Fall in love with yourself. It's the most important relationship you'll ever have in your life.

"If you're searching for that one person that will change your life, take a look in the mirror."
– Roman Price

15

Be Happy on Purpose

"The more you are in a state of gratitude,
the more you will attract things to be grateful for."
– Walt Disney

If you want to be happy, you absolutely, positively must be happy on purpose. Being happy isn't something that just "happens." It's not something that will just come to you effortlessly. It's something that you must work on and invest yourself in every single day.... especially on the days you don't feel like it.

It's so important that you reach the point in your life where you can recognize when you're not feeling so "happy," admit it, accept it, and then act to change it. Happiness isn't just something that occurs naturally and effortlessly. If it were, then we would all be happy all the time. Unfortunately, this isn't the case. It's also normal and ok for happiness to come and go. It's not an emotional state that is constantly occurring, as much as we hope for it to be.

Here are some things that you can start implementing and practicing in your life to be your happiest "you:"

1. Practice gratitude. Make a list of ten things that you are thankful for.

2. Spend time with people who make you feel good.

3. Do something you enjoy.

4. Smile for thirty seconds.

5. Listen to music.

6. Go for a walk in nature.

7. Look at pictures of moments when you felt happy before.

8. Go to a quiet place. Sit or lie down. Close your eyes. Ease your mind. Breath in slowly through your nose for five seconds. Hold for five seconds. Slowly release your breath through your mouth for five seconds. Repeat five times or until you feel relaxed.

9. Exercise.

10. Think of things that you would like to accomplish in the future.

Each of these things will change your emotional state. When you change your emotions, attention, and intentions, you'll automatically start to feel different; both positively and negatively. The more you practice this, you'll also notice that you'll be in this state of gratitude and happiness more often.

Remember, every situation that you face in life is temporary. So, when you're feeling happy, enjoy it fully and when you're not feeling so happy, remember that it won't last forever, and know that you have the power to change it.

Be happy on purpose.

16

The Price of Happiness

"If your happiness depends on money,
you will never be happy with yourself."
– Lao Tzu

So many people in society today live under the perception that such a thing as "happiness" can be purchased. I even fell for it. I'm not ashamed to say that I was one of those idiots who fell for it for almost a decade but, let's face it, this is what society teaches us.

This is what we see the second we turn on our televisions or unlock the screens of our smartphones. Advertisements telling us that we need to buy this to feel this. We need to go here to have this experience. We need to drink this beverage, so we can have fun with our friends. We need to buy a house like this, so our kids can smile like the kids in the commercials. We need to find a relationship on this website, so we can fall in love and live happily ever after.

So, tell me what do each of these things have in common? Think on it. Think hard. It's obvious but, apparently, it's something that we all are guilty of overseeing. Each of these things cost money.

Let's say you buy the product you saw in the commercials, you try it out, and you use it. Do you really feel as great as the paid actor or actress seemed to feel while they were using the product in the thirty second commercial you watched?

Did it really make a significant impact in your life? Yeah, I doubt it.

Society is teaching us that we need to buy our happiness when, in reality, this is so far from the truth. Happiness isn't something that can be purchased or ordered online. Love isn't something that you can just click a button and experience. A genuine smile isn't going to come across your face from purchasing what you watched on tv (I mean, unless it's Taco Bell or donuts. Those always make me smile.). There is no price for happiness. It can't be purchased. It can't be ordered. It can't be delivered to you in a box.

It took me nearly a decade, but I finally learned that if your happiness depends on money or objects, you'll never truly be happy. You will always want more. There will always be an insatiable void that you feel you must fill. It's inevitable.

If you want to find true happiness, you must first find self-love and gratitude. Happiness comes from within. It's as simple as that. No one or no thing can fill that void but you. It can't be purchased. It can't be generated from an object. It can't be generated from another person. It all starts with you.

One day, I came across this video by A Plus (2015) and it completely opened my mind. A handful of children were asked a series of questions regarding money and happiness. Their answers were so genuine, pure, and honest. The questions were:

1. Would you rather have all the money in the world and not have any friends or have a lot of friends and no money at all?

2. Would you rather be successful because you're rich or because you're happy?

The answers to question number one were all the same: *"Friends," "Definitely friends."* The answers to question number two were:

"Being [happy] with what I am instead of wanting something more. Sometimes, I am successful and sometimes I am not." (Smart kid!)

"Definitely happy."

"You can't buy happiness." (Bravo, kid! You get it.)

"I think success is just being happy with your life."

"Success means happiness."
(I couldn't have said it any better myself.)

Wow. Just wow. So, would you rather be rich or happy? That's the real question. It's a real eye opener. It's a concept so simple that even a child understands it; yet it seems so complex to us as adults.

Why? I'll tell you exactly why. Growing up, society taught us to go to school, get an education, get a job, get a car, get married, buy a house, and so on. They never taught us how to achieve happiness, love, healthy relationships, thriving friendships, or inner-peace. They should teach a course in grade school on inner-success rather than chemistry and calculus (which 90% of us probably won't ever use again in life).

I mean; let's be real here. As an adult, are you more likely to enter a relationship, struggle financially, and experience sadness or are you more likely to solve random calculus problems and use the periodic table of elements? I couldn't even tell you half of the shit I remember from the periodic table of elements, but I could easily tell you the first time I felt depressed and how I overcame it or the first heartbreak I had and how I eventually healed myself. This is what should be taught in school: how to achieve happiness and inner success.

As an adult, especially in this past year, I'm learning that there is so much more to this life than riches and success. I'll openly and honestly admit it; I had it wrong all this time. I was chasing the wrong things for almost a decade.

So, here I am today to try to prevent you from making the same painful mistakes that I made for so many years. Sometimes, we need to take a step back from our daily lives, jobs, stresses, and take a moment to breath and ask ourselves, "Am I really happy?"

Don't just ask yourself this once. Ask yourself often; as often as you can remember to. Set it as a reminder in your calendar. Put it in your Notes App on your phone. Put it on a sticky note. Just do it more than once. Way more than once. Maybe once a week or once a month.

Ask yourself, "Am I really happy?"

You'll probably be very surprised by the honest answer.

I know I was.

17

No Fucks Given

"The less fucks you give, the better you live."
– Anonymous

I'm so guilty of doing the exact opposite. I gave a fuck. I gave a ton of fucks. I spent most of my life caring too much about what others thought of me. My behavior for many years was dictated based upon the opinions of others; or better yet, my opinion of what I thought others' opinions were of me. Guilty as charged.

Not giving a fuck takes a shit ton of practice but, let me tell you something, once you're able to truly not give a fuck is when you'll finally feel free. You'll feel so empowered, invincible, and authentic. When you finally reach the point where you can just be yourself and live your life the way that you want to live it regardless of who's watching, that's when you're free. That's one of the best fucking feelings ever.

I get it though. It's tough. It's uncomfortable. It's intimidating. It's even scary sometimes. We all subconsciously fear rejection. Deep down, we all feel the need to be accepted by our peers, parents, mentors, friends, family, spouse, partner, etc. We fear being judged, ridiculed, and rejected.

But why? Why is it that we are so concerned with how others view us? Why are we so afraid to stand up for ourselves? To live our lives the way we want to? To take risks for ourselves? To chase our dreams? To experience our passions? To stand up for what we believe in? To go against the masses? Why the fuck are we such pussies?

I'll tell you why: overthinking. Instead of immediately acting on our natural impulses and intuition, we overthink our emotions and alter our behavior to conform to others' opinions and perceptions. We need to stop.

We need to start living each day as if it's our last. We need to start enjoying every moment that we have; the way we want to. We need to start appreciating every moment that passes us by because we don't know when our last moment will be.

Instead of overthinking, we need to start feeling and trusting our intuition when it tells us to act and respond. We need to start living our passions, chasing our dreams, standing up for our beliefs, and fulfilling our purposes. Fuck everyone else's opinions.

This is your life; not theirs. Stop giving a fuck about them and start giving a fuck about you.

#fuckwhattheythink

18

Don't Lose Yourself in a Relationship

"At some point, you have to develop healthy barriers for how you're going to be treated; you're responsible for your experience, nobody else is."
– Sylvester McNutt

Personally, I've had the unfortunate experience of "losing myself" in an unhealthy relationship for over eight years. The truth is: I had no one to blame but myself. I allowed it to happen. I tolerated it. I was responsible. I made a mistake. I learned, I grew, I left, and I moved on.

For years, I couldn't find the strength to stand up for myself and do what was right for me. I knew what I needed to do but I could never bring myself to do it. So many people would say, "Elina, you're such a strong woman. Why do you tolerate this?" "Elina, you deserve so much better. Why are you with him?" "Elina, you're way out of his league. What the fuck are you thinking?" "Elina, you can do this business without him. What are you doing?"

The fact was his voice was always louder than mine, his opinion was always stronger than mine, and his arguments were always more tumultuous and blatant than mine. He was always more eager to please others than I was. He always cared more about other peoples' perceptions, so, he tried harder to voice his opinion than I did. People responded to his behavior and he knew that. I knew that.

Honestly, I didn't care. I should have but I didn't. I just wanted to work. I just wanted to build my company and become successful. That's all that mattered to me at that point in my life so, for years, I just ignored him. I let him do his thing while I did mine. I ignored my pain, frustration, emptiness, loneliness, depression, anxiety, anger, and sadness. I ignored everything. I escaped into my work and ignored it all.

I was twenty years old when I met the man that I would eventually be married to for six years. I was young, ambitious, naïve, and oblivious to everything around me; he recognized that. He was much older than I was; twenty-two years older to be exact. He used the fact that I was hungry for success, wanted to start my own business, build my own career, travel the world, and experience the finer things in life to his advantage.

So, we became friends, I helped him with his company and he was there when I started my first company. Then, we merged the companies together and entered a "relationship." I, honestly, don't even like referring to it as a "relationship" or a "marriage" because that's so far from what I considered it to be. To me, we were friends and business partners; nothing more, nothing less.

When I tried to leave a few months later to pursue my business venture and vision on my own, I was faced with an ultimatum: give it all up or stay with him. I proposed the idea of us remaining business partners and continuing to build the companies together, but he wanted more.

At that time, I was so in love with the company. I was so proud of what I've already built and invested my time and energy into that I couldn't just let it go. So, I had a choice to make; marry him and keep the company going or walk away from it all. So, I married him.

Looking back now, I realize that I could have easily just said, "Ok. Fuck you. Bye." and continued working and building the company that I loved. It would have been just fine and as successful as ever but, at that time, I was young, naïve, inexperienced, and afraid of losing what I knew.

By that point, I had invested countless sleepless nights, endless hours, and an insane amount of energy into building a client base and our company's reputation. I had lost 90% of my friendships and I had also risked jeopardizing my relationships with my family because I was so entirely consumed by the company. The company was my obsession and I wasn't just going to let it go. That was my biggest fear and he knew exactly that.

So, I spent the next six years of my life in a deep and angry depression, isolated from friends and family, and the only escape I had was working on the company. I poured my heart and soul into it.

I spent endless hours sitting in the office behind a computer screen, traveling to different cities every weekend to produce events, studying our competitors, learning how to build our websites, teaching myself skills, learning programs, building presentations, networking, marketing, advertising, social media, design, databases, filing systems, training employees, managing employees, overcoming my fear of public speaking, learning how to host events on a microphone, learning how to run events backstage, all of it; I learned it all. I taught myself how to run a business. I learned how to build a company and how to operate it successfully day to day.

During these years, I forgot who I was. I was so used to hearing him try to tell me who I was, what I wanted, how I felt, and what I enjoyed that I subconsciously started to believe him. He used to tell me that I couldn't accomplish anything without him; I eventually believed him. He used to tell me that everything I had was because of him; I eventually believed him. He used to tell me that my friends didn't care about me and they just wanted to use me; I eventually believed him. Anytime I would get close to someone, he would tell me that they were trying to take advantage of me; I eventually believed him.

He didn't support my plans of wanting to start my own company that helps inspire others through motivational programs and inspirational speakers; I eventually believed him and gave up on it. He used to discredit my plans of becoming an author one day; I eventually believed him and gave up on it. He used to laugh at my plans of wanting to become an inspirational speaker one day (in fact, he said he could do it better than me); I eventually believed him and gave up on it.

I allowed this behavior to continue for years until, one day, I finally had enough. We were in Costa Rica at the time and I finally said, "Fuck this. I'm going to do this. I've wanted to do this for years." And I did it. He couldn't stop me anymore. Enough was enough. I left him in our villa, drove the golf cart down to the beach, and got in a fucking kayak. Then, I went exploring and walked the beach for miles. I went horseback riding in the jungle and in the mountains. I had the time of my life because I fucking deserved it and he wasn't going to stop me anymore.

That week in Costa Rica ended up changing the entire course of my life. I finally realized that he had no power or control over me. I could do what I wanted, and he couldn't do a fucking thing about it. He didn't have the courage to.

Once I stood up to him, he didn't know how to react. He couldn't stand up to me once I stood up for myself. I was in control now. I took my power back and there was nothing he could do about it. Everything changed that week. I finally had enough. It was time for a change. It was time for me to become me again.

I remember standing on the doorstep of our villa making a promise to myself as we left Costa Rica. I promised myself that I would embark on a personal journey to learning what it truly means to be happy and successful. I wasn't going to allow anyone to stand in my way any longer.

Success to me means accomplishing true happiness, self-connection, inner-peace, love, purpose, helping others, and self-worth. Looking around and reflecting on my life today, I see that all these things naturally and effortlessly made their way to me from that very moment in Costa Rica. All I had to do was trust the pain, trust the process, and believe that everything was going to be alright; and it was. It always will be.

I made the mistake of masking my problems and distracting myself with work. I never took the time to deal with the cause of the issue; I hid it and I tried to avoid it. I forgot who I was. I forgot how strong I was. I forgot how fun I was. I forgot how excited I was to do the things I loved to do. I forgot how to have friends. I forgot how to connect with my family. I forgot everything that I once was. I let another person tell me who I was and what I wanted. I allowed another person to influence my own opinion of myself.

You don't deserve to be with someone that you can't be yourself around. You don't deserve to be with someone who is belittling or demeaning. You don't deserve to be with someone who is always eager to be right or have the final word. You don't deserve to be with someone who doesn't allow you to enjoy your life. You don't deserve to be with someone who doesn't allow you to spend time with your friends or family. You don't deserve that.

You deserve to be in a relationship with a person who appreciates everything about you, someone who wants you for you, someone who wants to help you succeed, and someone who wants to watch you grow into the best version of you that there is.

You deserve to be loved; the right way.

19

Authenticity is Your Only True State

"You can't fake authenticity."
– Mark Schaefer

Above all else, always stay true to yourself. The world needs you to be your authentic self. And, quite frankly, you owe it to yourself to do just that. Be the person you are when no one is around. That is your true authentic state and the world needs more people who will step out of their comfort and do just that. The world needs more people that can find the courage to let go of who we think we're supposed to be or, better yet, who we think other people think we're supposed to be.

We need to stop living in the perception of other people's perception. We become so worried about what we think other people think of us that we lose our authentic selves trying to be this person that we think we should be based on an opinion that may or may not be existent in another person's mind.

We're all guilty of this. I spent many years of my life trying to be someone that I wasn't because I thought it was who other people wanted me to be when, in reality, other people just wanted me to be myself. However, I couldn't be myself because I was so caught up living in the perception of other people's perception. It's a vicious cycle that I see repeated in so many lives.

We need to stop living for other's approval and start living for ourselves. The world needs more people who will own who they are, own their self-worth, own their strength, own their identity, own their fears, own their vulnerability, own themselves for themselves and not for anyone else.

Do it for yourself. You are strong. You are smart. You are capable. You are empowered. You are confident. You are proud of who you are. You know what your potential is. You know what you want in life. You deserve to achieve everything it is that you desire.

You are confident, but not conceited. You are empowered, but not arrogant. You are strong, but not power driven. You are who you say you are. No one else holds that power besides you. What you tell yourself every single day will ultimately lead to who you become as a person. You're in control. You have the power. Take a hold of your self-worth and take a hold of your authentic self so that you can attract the type of life that you deserve.

Become present and aware in the way you speak to yourself. Positive and empowering self-talk is so incredibly crucial and critical to your growth. It is a skill that should be practiced daily throughout the day. You become what you think.

If you tell yourself enough times and often enough that you are worthy of happiness and success, then you will start to believe it. You will start to naturally attract it. It will become a reality because you'll be in that emotional and mental state. You'll start attracting circumstances, people, and opportunities into your life that lead to happiness and success. Know that you deserve the best and that no one can tell you otherwise.

You deserve to be happy in the way that you want to be happy, with who you want to be happy with; even if that means being happy alone. Being alone and enjoying your solitude is a superpower only a few can handle. If that's what makes you happy, then by all means, that is exactly what you deserve.

Know that you are worthy of becoming who you want to become, and you are worthy of achieving everything imaginable in your lifetime. You deserve it. Do it for you.

Do it authentically.

20

Turn Your Passions into Profit

"Instead of wondering when your next vacation is,
maybe you should set up a life you don't need to escape."
– Seth Godin

The bottom line is this: If you're doing what you love, you'll never have a case of the "Mondays." Excuse my French but I can't fucking stand it when I hear people complain about Mondays.

Monday isn't the day to be dreading getting back to work. Monday isn't the day that should drain you. Monday isn't the day that should make you feel like you hate your life. Monday is supposed to be the day that excites you to the fucking core to be back at your passion. Mondays should motivate you. Mondays should ignite you. Mondays should inspire you. Mondays should energize you.

If you're not excited to get back to work on Monday, you're doing it all wrong. If you're working five days a week, spending your time making plans and preparing for the weekend, you're doing it all wrong. If you're doing nothing but complaining and feeling sorry for yourself five days a week, you're doing it all wrong. If you're at work and all you can do is think of something that you'd rather be doing, guess what? You're doing it all wrong.

If you have a vision, a passion and a goal in mind, you should be posting #TGIM instead of #TGIF on the gram.

Mondays are the shit. Get hungry for Mondays. Mondays should become your obsession; an insatiable obsession to accomplish something you love, something you enjoy, something that sets your soul on fire.

Now, with that being said, I want you to stop what you're doing. Stop everything. Stop your thoughts. Stop your distractions. Stop thinking about what you want to eat later. Just stop. Put this book down and ask yourself this question:

"Do Mondays excite me?"

Seriously. Put the fucking book down, take a breath and ask yourself this question: *"Do Mondays excite me?"*

Well, do they? Be honest with yourself. What was your immediate response? What was the first intuitive response that came to your mind the moment you asked yourself this question; not the response that you had to think about. What was your initial reaction? There's no wrong answer to this question.

Do Mondays excite you? If you answered, "Yes," that's fucking awesome. Keep doing what you're doing. You're on to something. If you answered, "No," well.... let's work on changing that answer to a "Yes." We have some work to do.

Too many people end up spending a large percentage of their lifetime working a dead-end job doing something they don't enjoy just to earn a living. That's not what we're designed for. We weren't born into this world to just go to meaningless jobs every morning, be stressed out, feel sorry for ourselves, pay our bills, and die. What kind of life is that?

Let's put this into perspective. Let's say someone works from the time they are eighteen until they are sixty-seven assuming they are working a full-time job of 39.2 hours each week. According to Revise Sociology (2016), that equals 1,842 hours that they'll spend at work each year with 5 weeks of vacation time. This means that they will spend a total of 92,120 hours at work during their adult life. That's a lot of fucking hours to spend doing something you don't enjoy.

Not only are too many people spending a large percentage of their lifetime at a job they don't love; too many people are also suffering from stress, depression, anxiety, depreciating health, divorce, estranged relationships with their children, family members, friends and loved ones. Many, if not all, of these things probably derived from spending too much time at work doing something they don't really enjoy or have a passion for.

So, now, ask yourself this question again:
"Do Mondays excite me?"

When I was twenty years old, I was one of those people who hated Mondays, so I dropped out of college and quit my marketing career to take a chance on myself. During the next decade, I built multiple businesses around my passions and became very successful doing what I loved and enjoyed.

Anything in life is possible. If a fuck-up like me can do it, you can do it, too. Pick what you want in life. Focus on it. Work for it. Believe in yourself and don't stop thinking about it until it's yours. Watch as it starts to become reality.

My dreams, failures, obstacles, and life experiences have taught me that everything is possible. You can have everything in life that you want; you just need to have enough courage to go out and fucking get it.

#TGIM

21

0% Luck 100% Hustle

"Today, I will do what others won't so, tomorrow,
I can accomplish what others can't."
– Jerry Rice

You know what my biggest pet peeve is? When people say, "You got lucky." I'm sure you've experienced this at one point or another, as well. Excuse my French but what the fuck is it with people that make them automatically assume that someone's success happened by sheer coincidence or dumb "luck?" I say it's a reflection of their limitation and imagination to accomplish the very thing that they are criticizing and envying.

In my case, if anything, I was "unlucky," but I chose not to give up on myself and let my circumstances defeat me. And that's exactly what you're going to do, too. You're going to take every shitty situation that has happened to you, every shitty situation that you have allowed to hold you back, every shitty situation that has broken you, every shitty situation that you have survived through, and you're going to use that to fuel your goals moving forward. That's exactly what you're going to do.

To become successful, you must become obsessed. Hungry isn't good enough, you must be starving. Your goals must consume you. You don't have to know exactly how you're going to become successful; you just need to believe you will.

Work hard. Focus on your goals. Believe you are already a success and you will, inevitably, become successful. It's really that simple. It took me a decade of studying and practicing the Law of

Attraction to become the person I am today and to achieve the things that I achieved. Do these six things and I guarantee you that you'll accomplish so much more than you ever believed you were capable of:

1. Define your goal.
2. Believe in yourself.
3. Have a sense of urgency.
4. Ignore the negative opinions of others. Surround yourself with others on the same mission of growth, success, and positivity.
5. Be selfish for yourself.
6. Never give up.

When I started my first company, I was homeless, jobless, and broke. The average person didn't see that; they didn't care. They didn't see the years of sacrifice, heartache, depression, and restless ambition that it took to achieve financial success. They only saw what was on the present surface. They saw the superficial success of a thriving business, world travels, Instagram posts, big houses, big cars, unnecessarily expensive dinners and clothes, and so on.

Every entrepreneur, business owner, and professional out there knows that to start a business, it takes a lot of sacrifice, capital, hard work, heartache, defeat, loans, and debt. That doesn't sound like luck to me. That's straight hustle. That sounds like hunger, better yet, starvation, to succeed at something you're passionate about.

The next time you scroll past someone on social media who's living your #lifegoals or when you pass someone driving your #cargoals, don't say to yourself, "Damn, that person's lucky." Say to yourself, "Damn, that *will* be me one day. Not because I'll get lucky but because I'll work for it and *earn* it."

22

Make Progress or Make Excuses

"If it is important to you, you will find a way.
If not, you'll find an excuse."
– Daniel Decker

It doesn't matter if it's regarding your business, relationships, love, marriage, family, friendships, health, time, productivity, attitude, or future; you have two options that you will always face in life: 1. Make progress. 2. Make excuses.

So, what's it going to be? Are you going to take control of yourself and your outcome or are you just going to be one of those people who settles and continues living life always wondering, "What if?" It's not complicated. It's a simple choice. You only have two options. What's it going to be?

We all have the same twenty-four hours each day. How we decide to use them depends on us. For every excuse you make, I guarantee you that there is someone else out there overcoming their doubts and fears trying to figure out how to move forward and do the very thing that you are avoiding.

If you don't act now, they'll be the one living your #lifegoals. Don't let that happen. You owe it to yourself to live the life that you've always imagined; a life abundant with happiness, health, success, fulfilling relationships, friendships, financial freedom, and inner-peace. You deserve that.

Let me put this into perspective for you so you can see just how simple it really is. One hour is only 4% of your day. That's not much, is it? One hour. That's all it takes to follow your passion. That's all it takes to make a difference in your life. Enough excuses. Enough saying to yourself, "I'm too tired." Enough "I can't." Enough "I don't have the time." Enough "I'm not motivated." Enough "I can't afford it." Enough "I'm too fat." Enough "I hate the way I look." Enough "I'm so unhappy." Enough "I'm so broke." Enough, "I don't have the willpower." Enough.

"Earl Nightingale said many years ago that one hour per day of study in your chosen field was all it takes. One hour per day of study will put you at the top of your field within three years. Within five years you'll be a national authority. In seven years, you can be one of the best people in the world at what you do."
– Brian Tracy

The bottom line is this: Excuses are for people who don't really want to accomplish their goals. Excuses are for people who don't want it bad enough. Even if you work a full-time job, have a family or a busy schedule, you can still find an hour in your day somewhere (even if you need to break it up) to enhance yourself in some shape or form.

Follow your passion by learning more about it. Research other people who are successful in what you want to do. Listen to a motivational video or audio book in the car on your way to work or to drop off the kids. Read a book or listen to an audio book as you fall asleep each night. Watch or research educational and inspirational content as you fall asleep each night.

Robert Collier once said, *"Success is the sum of small efforts – repeated day in and day out."* One little step forward each day gets you closer and closer to your goal. Start with one hour. That's it.

You either want it or you don't. Gather enough courage to set out and start living your dreams. It's not going to be easy but it's going to be worth it. No more excuses. It's time to make progress. It's time to make a difference.

"Live a few years of your life like most people won't, so that you can spend the rest of your life like most people can't."
– Anonymous

23

Work Smarter Not Harder

"It's the will. Not the skill."
– Jim Tunney

It took me several years to master the skill of working "smarter," not just in business, but in all aspects of my life. I acquired it through years of experience, failure, success, trial, and error. I learned that it is not the amount of time or tasks that you put into your work that determines your level of success, but rather, it's the amount of energy and effort that you devote to your work and goals.

Years of owning and operating my own businesses taught me that I worked more efficiently, focused better, and accomplished more when I was in a certain state of mind. To do this, I had to take personal time for myself to re-charge. At first, I felt guilty and non-productive for taking time away from work until I realized how necessary this was for me to effectively accomplish my business goals.

When I would take an hour away from the office to go to the gym, do cardio outdoors, or just to lay on the floor in a quiet room and meditate; I found that, when I returned to the office, I was able to focus better and work more efficiently.

I was in a better mood. I was energized. I was balanced. My mind operated on an entirely different level. It finally made sense: maybe this is what it means to "work smarter not harder."

It's smarter to take time away from your work to focus on yourself, relax, clear your mind, re-energize, re-collect yourself, spend time alone, then, return to work and find that you're more productive and more aware of how to achieve your goals.

Working harder means pushing yourself to the limits, having your eyes set on a goal, stressing for endless hours until that goal is achieved, jumping from task to task without stopping, and not allowing yourself the necessary time to rest your mind and energy. This isn't healthy. Trust me. This is out of balance. This is a self-destructive and self-sabotaging cycle.

You're human. It's necessary to re-charge. If you don't re-charge, you will run on empty and running on empty means that your mind is not operating at the level that it needs to be for you to get the job done. Free your mind. Free your time. Take care of yourself; mentally, emotionally, spiritually, and physically. Then, return to your work and get the fucking job done.

Work smarter not harder. Energy is the deciding factor here. The more energy that you pour into what you're passionate about achieving, the faster it will become your reality. Sometimes, you need to disconnect in order to re-collect yourself.

24

Simple Steps to Success

"Who you are tomorrow begins with what you do today."
– Tim Fargo

Six simple steps to success:

1. Define your goal.
2. Believe in yourself.
3. Have a sense of urgency.
4. Ignore the negative opinions of others.
5. Be selfish for yourself.
6. Never give up.

Step 1: Define your goal.

Define what it is that you want. Define your priorities. Define your passions. Define yourself. Write down your goals and keep them somewhere you can see them every day. Tape them to your bathroom mirror, ceiling, rearview mirror, or desk. Set them as a "Daily Reminder" in your phone calendar; whatever works for you, do it. Read them every day and, when you read them, visualize yourself accomplishing them. Manifest them into reality.

Always, always, always go with your passions and trust your gut. Never ask yourself if it's realistic or not, and never listen to the negative opinions from others. Your mind and your energy are powerful tools. You can train both to accomplish anything you want in life.

You and only you have the power to create and alter your reality and, ultimately, your future. No one else; just you. Anything that you can conceive in your mind, you can eventually manifest into reality. Meaning that whatever you imagine, no matter how surreal or farfetched it may seem, it can and will become a reality if you take the necessary steps to making that happen. Define what you want. Believe that it can happen, and it will. Believe it with all that you are.

Step 2: Believe in yourself.

People that know they will succeed always do. It's called the Law of Attraction and I live by it. I've practiced it for nearly a decade and I owe all my success, knowledge, experience, and accomplishments to it. I held no degrees nor any prior business experience before I achieved my success in my twenties; I only had my self-belief, energy, and pure ambition. You master those three things and I guarantee you can achieve anything that you want.

When I was only eighteen years old, I attended a business convention in Detroit, Michigan. That day, I conceived a dream that would later change the entire course of my life. I envisioned myself traveling, inspiring people, and working from my laptop in different cities around the world. I had no idea what "exactly" it was that I wanted to do with my life or as a career; all I knew was that it had to include these three things and I believed that I would do it one day….and I did.

If you have a dream, chase it. Don't worry about how it's going to get done; just know that it will. Change your mindset; change your future. Believe in yourself.

Step 3: Have a sense of urgency.

When you have an inspired thought or a feeling to pursue something, it is crucial that you act on it immediately. Channel that inspired energy before it's gone. Action, energy, and productivity produce results.

If you're waiting for the right time to take action, it's now. Do it before someone else beats you to it. While you're contemplating your next move or waiting for your "moment," someone else is out there trying to make it happen for themselves. Don't wait for opportunity to come to you. Go out there and create it.

If you happen to come across an opportunity and you're not confident whether you should take it or not, take advantage of it anyway. Take advantage of the moment while it's in front of you because, chances are, you probably won't see it again. Most opportunities don't come twice.

If you fail, oh well. You're better off taking advantage of it and failing than you are passing it up, regretting it, and being haunted by the "what ifs." You never know what could happen. You just might surprise yourself.

Step 4: Ignore the negative opinions of others.

Don't ever let someone tell you that you can't do something; that's not their place. They have no right. You are the only person who determines how far you go in this life. You want to be successful; that's up to you. You want to be happy; that's up to you. Everything you want to do in life; that's up to you.

People will come and go, as will their opinions. Most will tell you you're insane for believing that you will accomplish your dream; let them. Some will laugh at you; let them. Some will talk about you behind your back; let them. Some will support you; let them. Very few will believe in you; let them. Hardly any will help you. Therefore, it is so important that you realize that accomplishing what it is that you seek in this life is entirely up to you.

Sure, they'll tell you that they want to see you happy and achieve everything that you've ever wanted; and some may mean it, but when it actually comes down to it, how many of them do you think will be around when you have absolutely nothing to offer anymore, or will encourage you when you feel like giving up, or will answer your calls in the late hours of the night when you're depressed, or will come over to your house to console you for hours or days at a time until you feel motivated and inspired again, or will sacrifice the long hard hours into building your business and vision?

If you have someone that will do these things in your life, hold on to them and never let them go. They are rare. Most people who you consider friends will go running as soon as circumstances become uncomfortable or no longer benefit them in some way.

Just remember: you must make the right choices for yourself. The ones who truly care for you will support you, strengthen you, and stand by your side while the ones who don't will fade away; and that's ok. You never needed them anyways. You always need you more than you need them. Don't lose yourself trying to please others and absolutely do not lose sight of your goals or your needs because you're concerned with seeking another person's approval.

Step 5: Be selfish for yourself.

Do the things that make you feel fulfilled; the things that excite you and bring you to life. Go where you feel most alive and surround yourself with the people and the ideas that bring out the best in you. Your focus should be to constantly become a better version of yourself and fulfill your purpose. Yours. No one else. It's your life; your decisions, your future, and your vision. It's ok to be selfish for the right reasons. Do it for you. You'll thank yourself later.

That's why it is so important that you stay focused on your goals and your purpose. That's why it is crucial that you build a healthy internal relationship with yourself. That's why it is so important that you don't let others' opinions negatively affect you or get you off track of going after what you want in life. You determine the direction of your story; no one else. It all comes down to you and how selfish you are willing to be for yourself.

Success isn't about the amount of money you earn; it's about staying true to yourself, your beliefs, your vision, and your passion. It's about living your life to your standards. It's about becoming who you are meant to be.

Go after what matters most to you regardless of how that appears to others. Believe in yourself and do what's right for you. It's ok to be selfish for your own growth and your own goals. It's your life. Stay true to what's best for you.

Step 6: Never give up.

There is no easy way to accomplishing success. There will be ups and downs; highs and lows. This is inevitable. You must understand that from the beginning. You will fail. You will lose. You will be disappointed. You will be embarrassed at times. That's ok. That's normal. Shit happens. You pick yourself back up. You learn. You grow. You keep going.

It's important to view each failure as an opportunity to learn and grow rather than as a defeat. Learn to heal yourself after each failure. You cannot be considered or labeled a 'failure' until you give up. So, don't give up. Keep going. Keep building. Keep fighting. Never give up on what you believe in or who you're becoming.

"You miss 100% of the shots you don't take."
– Michael Scott

25

Simple Reminders to Live By

"Life is really simple,
but we insist on making it complicated."
– Confucius

Life can get overwhelming, challenging, frustrating, and discouraging at times. Here are some simple little reminders to get you back on track and help you continue kicking ass on your journey in this thing we call *"life."*

"The secret of change is to focus all of your energy not on fighting the old, but on building the new."

- *Socrates*

"You don't drown by falling into water. You only drown if you stay there."

- *Zig Ziglar*

"An attitude of gratitude will change your entire perspective on life."

- *Anonymous*

"Who you will be in the next five years depends on three things:
1. The books you read.
2. The people you meet.
3. The choices you make."

- Bob and Emilie Barnes
From The 15 Minute Money Manager

"Happiness is an inside job. Don't assign anyone else that much power over your life."

- Mandy Hale

"If you want to know how rich you are, find out how many things you have that money cannot buy."

- Anonymous

"Don't chase love, money, or success. Become the best version of yourself and those things will chase you."

- Tony Gaskins

"Take a deep breath and remember who the fuck you are."

- Anonymous

"Don't worry about failures. Worry about the chances you miss when you don't even try."

- Jack Canfield

"Making mistakes is better than faking perfections."

- *Anonymous*

"If your happiness depends on money, you will never be happy with yourself."

- *Lao Tzu*

"When you want to succeed as bad as you want to breathe, then you'll be successful."

- *Eric Thomas*

"Replace 'what ifs' and 'should haves' with 'fuck yeahs' and 'no regrets."

- *Anonymous*

"It's never too late to be what you might have been."

- *George Elliot*

"Don't think too much. Just do what makes you happy."

- *Anonymous*

"What you think, you become. What you feel, you attract. What you imagine, you create."

- *Buddha*

"The happiest moments of your life will be the times that you make someone else happy."

- *Anonymous*

"The only thing standing between you and a goal is the time it takes to achieve it."

- *Jordan Belfort*

"All the success in the world means nothing without the right people in your life."

- *Anonymous*

"Never forget the days you prayed for the things you have now."

- *Anonymous*

"Not being where you want in life is ok. Doing nothing about it is not."

- *Anonymous*

"Always go with the choice that scares you the most because that's the one that is going to help you grow."

- *Caroline Myss*

"Ten years from now, make sure you can say that you chose your life, you didn't settle for it."

- *Mandy Hale*

"Never let small minds convince you that your dreams are too big."

- *Anonymous*

"Success is the sum of small efforts, repeated day in and day out."

- *Robert Collier*

"If it is important to you, you will find a way. If not, you'll find an excuse."

- *Anonymous*

"The struggle you're in today is developing the strength you need for tomorrow."

- *Robert Tew*

"Just be you, and if people don't like it, well, fuck them."

- *Anonymous*

26

The 4-Year-Old Survivor: The Story of Charmion Janae

"Throughout our lives we are faced with many experiences that influence us and help shape us into the person we will become."
– Charmion Janae

This is a story that will move you. It completely moved me. This is a story of a true survivor who found the strength and the courage to keep fighting forward in life despite her circumstances and childhood trauma. That is true bravery. I can't even begin to explain how much I admire Charmion's courage to not only survive, but to rise, thrive, and grow into a happy, loving, and strong woman, wife, and mother to two beautiful children. That is true strength.

Here is Charmion's Story.

Elina: I'd love to hear about your story, Charmion. Who is the 4-year-old survivor that you mention?

Charmion: Throughout our lives we are faced with many experiences that influence us and help shape us into the person we will become. I close my eyes and I am there. Four years old, white t-shirt and blue jean overalls. I am walking up the stairs to play the game my uncle said would be so fun. As I climbed up the last step and peered down the hallway, I saw there was a light on in one of the bedrooms. I peeked around the corner of the doorway and saw my uncle sitting at the edge of the bed. He told me to come in and close the door. From that moment on, it mostly becomes a blur, but I remember him undressing me, and then he started to touch me and proceeded to rape me.

Elina: Wow. This literally makes my heart stop. I'm at a loss for words.

Charmion: This happened many times and everyone in the family knew about the abuse, but no one cared enough to save me. A few years before this incident, my sister was beaten to death at the hands of family friends who were given guardianship of my siblings and me. To this day, my brothers still blame themselves for her death, though they have scars from their attempts to save her.

Elina: Wow. I honestly don't know what to say. I'm so sorry for all that you've been through. When I look at you, I see this happy, vibrant, beautiful woman with so much life, energy, and positivity in her. It's so hard to imagine that these are the experiences that you've lived through. You truly are a survivor. I admire you. It takes a tremendous amount of strength and courage to endure what you've been through, yet alone, be able to find the strength to share it with others.

Tell me more about your parents. When were you placed in the system?

Charmion: At the time, my parents were in and out of jail for drug related problems. When they found out about the tragic death of my sister, they acted as any grieving parent would; they both self-medicated. My mother was no longer my mother. The crack she used to numb the pain had taken over her mind, body, and soul.

When I say the crack has taken over her mind; it was to the point that she asked me how to spell my name, and she was the one who named me. When I say it has taken over her soul; sometimes when she called, she would ask for money and when it was not given to her, she would say she is glad she gave us up for adoption.

Elina: Wow. What happened next?

Charmion: After the abuse, starvation, and neglect we endured from our aunt and uncle, CPS was notified. I remember the day the police came. They told us we had to be very quick and handed us black trash bags to pack up our belongings. I was five. A lady cop helped me gather my stuff, and as I look back now, I know why there was such sadness in her eyes.

After being separated from my older brothers, we were placed into the system, each feeling scared and alone. I found myself sent to various foster and children's homes. Some of the foster homes were not kind to me. Finally, when I was seven, I was adopted with one of my older brothers into the new family.

Elina: How did you like the new family?

Charmion: For the first time since being put in the foster system, I felt loved and safe. The new family had three biological sons of their own, and adopted not only me and my older brother, but also four other children. The new family taught me everything! How to eat with utensils, tie my shoes, read, and much more. My adopted dad was a pastor, so, I was able to learn about God and how awesome He is.

Elina: When did you first discover that you had Sickle Cell?

Charmion: When I was sixteen, I started having a lot of abnormal bleeding and was eventually hospitalized. In order to live, your hemoglobin count is supposed to be between fourteen and twenty-four. Mine had dropped to five, which is critical.

Being adopted, my medical records were lost in the transitions, and we did not know that I had the Sickle Cell Trait which was acting like the disease. I was given a blood transfusion, sent to multiple doctors, and sent home with various medications.

Elina: What happened next?

Charmion: One of the medications was a sleeping pill which the doctor thought would help preserve my energy because I was so tired. While on the sleeping pill, I found myself waking up naked, panty-less, with my pajamas missing when I had gone to bed with all those items on. I also woke up hurting and swollen down there. My doctors and I just thought it was due to my Sickle Cell. Unfortunately, this would go on for three more years.

It wasn't until I was nineteen and pieced everything together that I learned all those things were due to me being raped in my sleep by one of my adopted parents' biological sons. Upon finding this out, I went to my sisters to tell them what I suspected, and one of them had the same story. She, too, found herself waking up naked and hurt. She later revealed that this brother would assault her during the day, as well, and had threatened her to keep her from telling anyone.

My sisters and I went to our parents; me with my suspicions that I thought this brother was doing something to me, and my sister with actual proof and knowledge that this brother was her assailant.

My parents went to their real son and confronted him, and he admitted to everything. My sisters and I were then asked to keep quiet; they were going to get him counseling. They said that if we said what he did affected us in any way, it was for attention.

My dad, the pastor, went to the elders of the church to tell them the news before it could come out in the town newspaper. The problem was that these elders left telling a totally different story. They told their families and the other people in town that me and my sisters were troubled and had wanted it.

I was asleep when all this was done to me, but I soon found myself sitting in a pew alone and hearing the whispers and rumors. I left my childhood church to find a new one. I was going crazy trying to clear my name around town and prove that I was a victim. I never wanted anything except for everyone to know the truth. Then my adopted family started picking sides. They picked his.

I was told I needed to forgive and move on. Those dismissing words, the rumors, and having no one to support me were the reasons why I tried, unsuccessfully, to end my life. My assailant only got one hundred days of probation after admitting everything to the police. That is what happens when your father is a well-known pastor in a small town.

Elina: Wow. Just wow. Your story is so powerful and literally makes it hard for me to breath. You are such a strong woman to have survived all of this. I admire your courage and strength to continue to be so positive and have such a bright outlook on life;

even after all that you've been through. How did these events immediately effect you and how were you able to find the strength within yourself to grow into the positive and loving woman you are today?

Charmion: From that moment on, I went into a downward spiral. I turned to alcohol and partying to try to shut out the pain. I had always questioned my worth because I felt if my biological parents didn't want me, there must be something wrong with me. When my adopted family did the same thing, I knew I was not worthy of anyone's love. I had tried to prove, in everything I did, that I was worth something. But these important people in my life did not agree, or at least so it seemed.

I had been given up by not one set of parents, but two. I was left abandoned by my birth family and my adopted family, by a church and a town, which left me depressed and asking; who will I be? How will I survive all of this too?

I am that 4-year-old survivor, now twenty-three. I have moved past all the pain and tragedy to find happiness; I forgave all the people who wronged me. I went on to get married and became a mother of two beautiful children. I model, and plan to attend a dental program.

I am surrounded by people who love me, and I no longer have to try to prove to anyone I am worth anything because, now, I know my worth! I am awesome. I am beautiful. I am loved. Those rumors did not destroy me. My past does not define me. The people who gave me up and walked away from me when I was in need will not hinder me from future love and friendships being made.

Elina: What advice would you give to someone who feels like giving up right now?

Charmion: Don't! Hard times can be like a dark tunnel. There is light at the end but, in that moment or tragedy, all you feel is the darkness. I promise if you keep moving forward, the light gets brighter and, eventually, there will be daylight.

Elina: In closing, if you could leave your children with three lessons, what would they be?

Charmion:

1. To never lose themselves in this world trying to be someone or something they are not.

2. Anything is possible if you work hard.

3. Always forgive because life is hard enough and too short to dwell on things that are out of your control.

"Strength does not come from winning. Your struggles develop your strengths. When you go through hardships and decide not to surrender, that is strength."
– Arnold Schwarzenegger

27

You're a Diamond, Dear. Nothing Can Break You.: The Story of Renecka Ross

"A diamond doesn't start out polished and shining.
It once was nothing special, but with enough
pressure and time, becomes spectacular."
– Solange Nicole

Author, motivational speaker, mentor, mother, and humanitarian. Becoming a mother at the age of fourteen, she was determined to succeed and not become another statistic.

Meet Renecka Ross, founder and president of *#diamondsaresetapart*, a non-profit organization focused on reminding young girls of their worth and pushing them toward their purpose. Her challenging past of fear, low self-esteem, and becoming a young mother compelled her to start a positive movement geared toward teen girls.

Each year, Renecka holds a purity banquet for young girls and their parents where vows are exchanged. This evening event includes a catered dinner, desert, and a program ceremony specially dedicated to each girl. Renecka's life motto is: "To remind every teen girl that diamonds are surely set apart, and each one of them is destined for greatness."

During the past several years, Renecka found the strength and courage within herself to step out on fulfilling her purpose by mentoring teen girls. Her dream is to, one day, open a group home for young girls and travel the world; leaving the notion that anything is possible if you just believe in yourself.

Renecka believes that your past doesn't define you but can be used as a stepping stone to push you toward your destined future. She has just successfully completed her Human Resources Management Certification, as well as, writing her first book, *"Dear Diamond.*" Her everyday goal is to touch the life of at least one person.

Here is Renecka's Story:

Elina: Thank you for being a part of The Inner Success Project's *#SHAREYOURSTORY*. Tell me a little bit about yourself, Renecka.

Renecka: My name is Renecka Ross and I am the mother of two amazing boys. My life is no fairytale but everything I have went through has made me the woman I am today.

I became a mom at fourteen years old. I was a teen that suffered from low self-esteem. At times, I wondered why I was living and couldn't understand why I was chosen to go through so much. I wasn't a teen that fit in with everyone. I was an honor roll student, quiet at times, and didn't think I was the prettiest girl to look at.

I never really knew my biological dad, which is why I feel that I searched for love in all the wrong places. As young girls, we always want to be daddy's little princess, but without a dad, this fairytale kind of fades away. I just really wanted to be loved, really wanted to be accepted, and for some reason, I just knew I was different.

My granddad was my life. He tried his best to convince me that I was destined for greatness. Instead, life threw me so many curve balls that I just felt like giving up. You see, society was determined to convince me that I was a failure, that I would never graduate Junior High School, yet go to high school, and graduate on time.

Elina: Well, you most certainly are not a failure. The movement that you have created and the lives that you have changed are so inspiring. That is a strong and pure definition of success. I'd love to hear more about your story of becoming a mother at such a young age. I became a mother at a young age, as well, and it always fascinates me to come across other young mothers who took their circumstance and used it to create a better future. It's such a beautiful thing.

Renecka: During my early months of pregnancy, I lived with a pen pal of mine who pushed me to finish school. Between her and my granddad, they picked my work up from my teachers and I finished my eighth-grade year with an honor roll GPA. Back then, they didn't have home schooling, so, I had to teach myself. I had to read and study a lot because it was on me to make it for my unborn son.

I worried if I would be able to love my son or give him the best life because I struggled behind a mask that hid a lot of my pain. I didn't know that God made me special, that I was destined to be different, or that He loved me despite anything; and to Him, I was indeed special.

Between being a teen, learning to be a mom, finishing school, and working when I was able, I still struggled with loving myself.

I found it hard to trust. I didn't want to talk about how I felt, and I buried myself in books.

Elina: What has been one of the most powerful and impactful experiences throughout your life?

Renecka: I lost my auntie at a very young age from breast cancer. She was my very first best friend, my confident, and a love that I will carry forever. Losing her really made me feel alone, and I struggled with her loss for a very long time. That was the moment I realized that death was real and that every moment of life counts.

Elina: You truly have an incredible story. I'm so sorry for your loss. If you don't mind me asking, I'd love to hear more about your depression and the ways you overcame it.

Renecka: Depression is so real, and I thank God that I overcame it. You don't have to be in the streets to make mistakes or a teen drop out. I was an honor roll student, a part of "Breakfast for the Champions," and won numerous essay contests; yet none of the above made me realize that I was truly different and set apart.

I went through so much and overcame some obstacles; I owe it all to God. You see, He had to reintroduce me to myself. He assured me that I was a diamond and I was set apart for greatness. Then, He later showed me why I endured so much.

I used to live my life allowing guys to tell me anything, compressing myself for love, and running away from purpose. This all changed when I recognized how special I was to God. He placed so many amazing women in my life to coach me, encourage me, and see myself above what naysayers said I would become.

Elina: That's a beautiful response. So, you've successfully grown into this incredibly brilliant business woman. I'd love to hear more about the vision and impact of your organizations.

Renecka: Today, I am the CEO of two organizations. They are entitled, *#diamondsaresetpart*, and *2 Above and Beyond.* These organizations have given my testimony a voice.

I operate more in *#diamondsaresetapart.* This is an organization where I mentor young girls and teen girls; some with kids and some without. I also speak at schools, youth conferences, and events.

Every year, I have a purity banquet where as many as one hundred girls come together with their parents and are presented with a jewel that will be replaced one day by their husband. I remind them that their bodies are a temple and that God created them to be diamonds. I hold different conferences, pajama parties, one on one mentoring, and many other exciting things, as well.

I have been interviewed by radio stations, known by many teen girls, and well respected by my purpose. The blessing is that I have been where a lot of these girls are. I not only mentor them, but I talk to their moms, too. I tell them signs to look for and ways to connect with their girls. No matter how old women are, they will always need their mom.

I have seen a lot of my diamonds, which I like to call them, graduate from college and now working some fantastic jobs. I am like a quiet voice for these young girls. When they hear my story, they always look at me funny because I look nothing like what I have been through.

I have survived being homeless, being addicted to sleeping pills, and suffering from depression. Everything I went through was for a reason; not to help me, but to encourage girls all around the globe. My constant prayer is for God to take me global.

Elina: This amazes me. You amaze me. Your generosity and humility are truly something special. What is something great and positive that has happened in your life recently?

Renecka: I am currently completing my first book and recently completed my Human Resources Management Certification. Did I mention, God blessed me with a dad? My mom's ex-husband, who has been around since I birthed my oldest son, has recently asked to adopt me. Yes, I am a grown thirty-seven-year-old woman going through an adoption and I am super excited.

Elina: This makes my heart smile! Congratulations! I am so happy to hear this. So, what's next for you?

Renecka: To continue to touch the lives of as many young girls and women as I can, while using my purpose as a voice. Concluding with my ultimate dream and legacy, which is to own two group homes for teen girls and to encourage them to succeed in all areas of life.

Elina: What has struggle taught you?

Renecka: Every struggle has taught me to be humble and every tear has taught me to love life more and more. I believe my purpose lies in each young girl that I meet, and the blessing is them trusting me and pushing to do their best.

Elina: What advice would you give to someone who feels like giving up right now?

Renecka: No matter what tomorrow will bring, dig deep down inside of you and pull up as much strength that you ever could imagine.

Throughout life, there will be valleys, as well as, storms you may be faced with, trust me when I say that God will carry you through. You never know how strong you are until you have to push your way through an obstacle or until you have to face your weakest moments you just feel enough is enough.

Life will throw you curve balls, but faith will hand you the biggest bat to hit them and land on a home plate labeled, "Overcomer."

You are more than enough, built to last the toughest storms, and bold enough to declare a victory. Don't lose faith, and don't give up, you were built for this! Begin to speak life in every situation and see yourself making it through, up until the day of manifestation.

Elina: If you could leave your children with three lessons, what would they be?

Renecka: If I could leave my kids with three lessons they would be:

1. Stand on your faith through all things.

2. Don't regret mistakes, instead consider them as life lessons, when choosing to do better.

3. Dare to be different and fulfill your purpose with boldness.

Elina: In closing, what fulfills you?

Renecka: If I can save the life of just a few young girls, I can honestly leave this place feeling that my purpose has been fulfilled.

"Difficult roads often lead to beautiful destinations."
– Zig Ziglar

28

The Vegan Superwoman: The Story of Connie Chi

"When everything seems to be going against you, remember that the airplane takes off against the wind, not with it."
– Henry Ford

Trilingual, brilliant, vegan, survivor, superwoman. I'd like for you to meet Connie Chi. Connie's story is one of true strength and resilience. Connie is a successful self-made business woman, and the founder and CEO of *The Chi Group*, a global branding agency. She also hosts a podcast called, *"The Brand Academy Podcast."* Connie's work has been featured and mentioned in numerous media outlets including Buzzfeed, Elite Daily, Business Insider, CEO World Magazine, and multiple others.

Connie has seen it all, from starting her own companies, continuing to succeed after three failed businesses, surviving a near-death-experience, and rebuilding her entire life while finding herself, her strength, her motivation, and her enormous courage to never give up no matter what.

Here is Connie's Story.

Elina: So, tell me a little bit about yourself and your story.

Connie: My name is Connie Chi, founder + CEO of *The Chi Group*, a global branding agency humanizing and co-branding brands. I've had three failed businesses in the past and, in addition to that, about four years ago, I almost lost my life as my ex nearly killed me.

I was stalked on social media and in person which forced me to move out of New York City and be put under an address confidentiality program for my safety. I lost everything from my cushy New York City corporate ad sales job, my savings, my Manhattan apartment, and my friends.

Not only did I have to wipe myself off all social media for a few years, I had Facebook blackball me since my ex was impersonating me and used my photo to solicit sex on various sex websites.

Elina: Wow. That's insane to have to go through all of that. How did this situation effect you?

Connie: The experience was extremely humbling and, never in a million years, did I think I would be going through something like that in my thirties. Naturally, I said to myself, "I'm a college educated woman with good credit who never once got a speeding ticket, none the less, any run-ins with the law."

Elina: So, what happened next? How were you able to pick yourself back up and just start "living life" again?

Connie: It took a really supportive lawyer, family, and lots of therapy to get to the point that I am at now regaining trust in, not just men, but also in humanity.

Being that I run a business and have to be the face of my company, it's definitely a huge step to getting back onto social media. My story was written about in The New Yorker Mag and I had a video interview done by Broadly.

Elina: That's incredible. I applaud you for your strength and courage. What advice would you give to someone who feels like giving up right now?

Connie: Life is extremely precious and, in those moments, when we feel like giving up, you need to ask yourself what is the opportunity? In our darkest moments, it's easier to just throw in the towel, but what if you didn't? What if you didn't throw in the towel and you were able to change someone else's life?

Elina: Earlier, you spoke on how your ex nearly killed you. I've personally dealt with a stalker in my past and had to start over because of it, as well, not nearly on the level that you have I'm sure but, regardless, that's a very scary situation to live through. How did you overcome that?

Connie: Honestly, it was therapy which really kick-started the healing process for me and really having the courage to take one small step towards living life again. Even today, I still have my struggles, but it's when we're brave enough to have faith that there's someone up above watching out for us. It keeps me going.

Elina: Now, you're this incredibly successful self-made business woman. What were your greatest motivators when starting your first business?

Connie: I was tired of working on other people's dreams and, when I went through my horrific situation, I realized how much you cannot depend on someone else to bring joy to your life. It needs to start with you first, even in business.

Elina: What were your greatest struggles when starting your first business?

Connie: I went through so many: fear of not being enough, fear of failure, and whether I could take another blow to my self-esteem if I failed to succeed.

Elina: As an entrepreneur myself, I understand how challenging it can be to push yourself to keep going all the time. How did you motivate yourself when you were feeling discouraged?

Connie: I was fortunate enough to have been exposed to a lot of personal growth mentors, whether it was Tony Robbins, Les Brown, Brendon Burchard, Jim Kwik, and more.

In those moments when I felt discouraged, I would play their videos every night and listen to it until I fell asleep.

Other times, I would disconnect from the world and do personal inventory on what has gone right in my life, being grateful for what I already have, and analyzing what/who I need to purge in order to get myself closer to my goals.

Elina: That's beautiful. We have so much in common. I practice the same things myself. It truly makes all the difference. In closing, if you could leave the world with three lessons, what would they be?

Connie: This is such a GREAT QUESTION!

1. Love like you never loved before.

2. Learn the art of forgiveness for others and yourself.

3. There's always an opportunity, even in the painful moments.

"The one who falls and gets up is so
much stronger than the one who never fell."
– Roy T. Bennett

29

The Struggle is Real: The Story of Robby D'Angelo

"The struggle you're in today is developing the strength you need for tomorrow."
– Robert Tew

Meet Robby D'Angelo: Best-selling author of the book, *The Struggle is Real*, founder of *RISE UP Health Initiative,* and host of *The Biohacked Life* podcast. Robby's incredible weight loss transformation of losing one hundred and fifteen pounds, fulfilling his life-long dream of playing college football, being featured in the number one men's health magazine in the market, competing on stage in a men's physique competition, and overcoming numerous mental and emotional obstacles throughout his lifetime is truly inspirational and empowering.

Here is Robby's story:

Elina: It was a pleasure hearing you speak as you shared your story during the *INSPIRE ME* luncheon in Biloxi, Mississippi. I always enjoy following your inspirational posts and your personal journey on social media, as well. Always so positive! I'm already familiar with your story but I'd love for you to share your incredible transformation with our readers. I'd also love to hear more about *The Biohacked Life* and *RISE UP Health Initiative* and how it has helped to transform and inspire so many lives.

Robby: *The Biohacked Life* is the evolution of my years of coaching. I started out just doing nutrition and exercise, but after a couple years of being more psychiatrist than health coach, I realized it was more about mental health than physical health.

After all, your physical health starts on the inside with your mind and heart. I am an absolute nerd with everything involving human potential from psychology and philosophy to the study of nutrigenomics and epigenetics. I love learning about all the ways I can serve those around me to become the best version of themselves. The first thing I do every morning, after my coffee of course, is to read all the new published research on human optimization.

RISE UP is really my ultimate passion. Everything I do in life is for the ultimate goal of devoting my 100% to *RISE UP*, which promotes mental health in schools.

Much like my coaching journey, I started out working in schools promoting positive eating habits and the importance of being active, but after tons of work, I saw that, more than anything, these kids were struggling with mental health.

My main message in the schools is to give kids hope in realizing they do not have to be the victim. Their current circumstances don't define who they are or who they will be. It's just a scene in the story of life they are writing with every choice they make.

I also encourage them to be the light in a dark world. There is so much negativity surrounding them, and they have an incredible opportunity to be the hero their community needs them to be.

Elina: Amazing. So, tell me more about your struggles with your weight as a child and how it led to your transformative journey.

Robby: As far back as I can remember, I have always struggled with my weight and food. Some of my earliest memories involved being unhealthy and overweight. Growing up like most of America, I was never educated in making proper nutritional choices.

Being just a kid, I was unable to analyze why I binged to the point of misery. I now understand that I, too, was using food to compensate for something missing in my life. Many people say they are filling a void or food makes them happy.

In elementary school, I was always known as the "fat kid" and was often left out of activities I could see everyone else enjoying. As a result, I became very shy and introverted.

Growing up, my entire family excelled in athletics. I also grew up watching my older brother follow in their footsteps by becoming a star athlete in every sport he attempted. Then there was me, the chubby kid that always lagged behind. I would watch him and say to myself, "One day, I will be a great athlete just like him." He had the talent and athleticism I desperately wanted.

Growing up in that high-pressure environment, I became very insecure. I was struggling so much with my negative body image and insecurities, that I was almost too embarrassed to be out in public.

In order for me to find acceptance, I thought I had to become this overly "nice guy." In my head, I had to go above and beyond to please people because I had to make up for my negative body image. I would let people walk all over me and I would never even think of being assertive. I lacked confidence in who I was, so, I overcompensated. The "nice guy" mentality carried with me for most of my life because, like most people, I wanted to fit in and be accepted; to me, that was the only way I could.

Elina: So, when did it all begin to change for you? What brought you to finally take that first step to embark on this journey?

Robby: I was tired of not being able to be the real me because I was trapped within the walls of negativity I built around me. I had developed so many coping and defense mechanisms to shield myself from the world around me instead of dealing with the problem at the root of it all: my weight.

At this time of being sick and tired of being sick and tired, I finally made the decision to drop the weight. The transition from eating everything in sight to eating calorie conscious foods was tough at first. I often had this insatiable hunger that would just not go away even after a large meal.

When the negative thoughts attacked me, it would bring on a plethora of negative emotions that left me feeling depressed and hopeless. The mental battles one goes through is, in my opinion, the hardest part of any transformation.

After I had lost a few pounds, it gave me the confidence I needed to give sports the effort needed to excel. It was during my weight loss that I developed my love for football. It gave me another reason to eat healthier and get in shape. I got in shape for athletics and was finally healthy and fit.

With the weight loss, I finally had the confidence in myself to break down those mental walls and start letting the real me out. I was socially more acceptable, and I was gaining happiness with myself. The positive self-image and confidence I gained during my initial weight loss was only temporary though.

Elina: How so?

Robby: I came to a crossroads in my life. I was faced with one of the first major decisions I had to make regarding my future and I struggled to find my answer. It had always been my dream to play college football like my dad and to be a star athlete like my brother. I saw the way people revered them for their accomplishments, and I wanted to experience that.

The problem was in the decision that lied in front of me. I could continue my new healthy lifestyle, stay skinny, and, with tons of hard work, have a small chance of playing on the next level, or I could get big again and increase my odds of attaining my dream of being a college athlete.

I put in so much time and effort in losing weight, but I knew the probability of becoming a college athlete would be greater if I could drastically increase my size. I wanted both: to be lean and to play football.

Elina: So, which did you choose?

Robby: I chose my dream. I went back to my ways of binge-eating everything in front of me. I would eat anything I could get my hands on just to gain weight for football. In my head, I now had a purpose for binge-eating. I took away the negative association with over-eating and gave it justification.

I put on roughly twenty pounds each year of my high school career and graduated at 6'2" and 285 pounds. Even though, I was having huge success on the football field becoming a High School All-American during my senior year, in my head, I was once again dealing with overwhelming insecurities because of my weight.

As I started my collegiate career, I was in a better situation but still eating unhealthily. I was built like a big, strong power-lifter, but struggled to gain as much weight as I needed to excel at my position.

I played offensive line in college, mainly the venter position. Even though, I was a compulsive binge-eater, I was constantly fluctuating about thirty pounds each year. I would literally wake up every morning and make myself a 2500-calorie protein shake just to start my day. That's more calories than most people consume in an entire day. I was constantly tired, lethargic, and still expected to perform at a high level.

With finding success on the field and being the massive strong guy on the team, I had many people watching me and looking up to me. Experiencing that part was great, but inside of me, all I could think about was wanting to, once more, get rid of the weight. I was one of the most recognized athletes on the team yet still felt empty inside.

My body had never gotten the proper nutrition it needed and after years of all-out abuse from practice and pushing myself in the weight-room, it was now catching up with me. My body started physically declining and my knees started weakening.

During my senior year of college football, I was 6'2" and 305 pounds. I achieved my life-long dream of playing college football, but it came with a price. I endured four knee surgeries within a year along with numerous other injuries including a broken shoulder. Needless to say, my body was telling me, "No more," and I had to come to the conclusion that I had no chance of playing in the NFL.

Elina: Where did your weight loss journey lead you to next?

Robby: Two years later, I have the best body I have ever had and accomplished something I never thought I could achieve; I had visible abs. I know it is just superficial but, to me, it means so much more. It represents all the hard work and determination that it took to take my 305-pound body down to 190 pounds. It represents perseverance of making it through the struggle and the negativity inside of me.

As a first-ever crowning achievement, I did my first-ever professional photo shoot for a supplement company that chose me to be one of their sponsored athletes. Then, I found out that the ad for the supplement company would be placed in the number one men's health magazine in the market. I finally am one of those "fit guys" that I never thought was possible.

I also stepped out of my comfort zone to compete on stage, actually in front of people and judges, in a men's physique competition. I made it a point to do this to challenge and overcome my negative body image. To go from someone that used to not take his shirt off at the beach to now being judged by your body alone was a huge mental challenge for me.

The competition was not for vanity, so I can show off my body; for me, it was to mentally get past all the negativity surrounding the way I used to see myself. I ended up placing third and I could not have been more pleased.

I set a goal, gave it everything I could, and finished it.

Elina: Wow! What an incredible transformation! Congratulations! I'm sure that accomplishment was so very rewarding. What has this journey taught you and how has it affected you intrinsically?

Robby: I believe we must understand the past in order to know what we want in the future. I can look back and know that I am admittedly 100% the product of my past and the choices I have made.

With small fluctuations here and there, I have managed to keep the weight off for ten years now and I am even more passionate about the health and fitness lifestyle than ever before.

I often get asked how I accomplished my transformation, so, I tell my story with passion and conviction because I hope it inspires others. I have managed to lose and keep off one hundred and fifteen pounds.

For the first time in my life, I am 100% authentic to who I want to be and the feeling of joy that has come from that is unexplainable. I am extremely grateful for the struggles I have been through because without them, I would not truly understand my own strength to overcome. I feel every individual deserves to, deep down, feel good about where they come from, who they are, and where they are heading in life.

Elina: What advice would you give to someone who feels like giving up right now?

Robby: Step one: BREATHE! Get back to gratitude and remember your "Why!" Why is your journey important? Who are you doing this for?

During my deepest depression where I was to the point of giving up on life and calling it quits, I thought a lot about the meaning of life. Why am I here? By getting back to a state of gratitude, I was able to remind myself, "My purpose is so much bigger than my insecurities!"

After that, I just started setting one small goal a day. I had to get my confidence back and the best way I knew to do that was by setting small daily goals.

For instance, my first goal coming out of my last bad depression was to just show up at the gym. I didn't have to work out or do anything; JUST SHOW UP! After I made that a routine, of course, I started to work out harder and harder.

Then, I built upon that and integrated healthier eating and started listening to personal growth books on my phone. I made it a point to have small victories every day because I had to prove to myself that I could set goals and actually accomplish them. Those small victories started rewriting my broken internal story and it proved to myself that I was not the loser I said I was.

Elina: One thing that we surely have in common is that we're both introverts by nature. What I've noticed, tough, is that those insecurities suddenly disappear and we both come alive when we're standing on stage, coaching, inspiring, or helping others. How did you initially find the courage or the motivation to become a speaker, coach, and overcome your introvert tendencies?

Robby: It's simple. My passion for helping others is so much stronger than my insecurities. No matter how uncomfortable I am, I set my thoughts on powerfully serving. My internal dialogue goes from: "What are they thinking about me? Maybe I'm not good enough." to "I am going to serve this person with every ounce of energy inside of me." I take my thought from my ego to being in service of someone else.

Elina: What has been one of the most powerful and impactful experiences throughout your life?

Robby: The journey to self-awareness that I gained through writing my book. It made me do the deep work on myself to fully understand why I do the things I do in my life. When I first wrote my story in the book, I was thirty years old and boiled down my entire life to a page. I sat back and thought to myself, "This is sad."

During the book writing process, I interviewed over one hundred people to gain a better understanding of other peoples' perspectives. While conducting those interviews, I became really good at asking questions. I simply turned those questions on myself to better understand the underlying reasons and motivations behind all the decisions I made throughout my life.

For the first time, I knew my emotional eating triggers. I knew why some things triggered me to snap and why some things led me to making bad decisions. The understanding of self-awareness is the single most important thing I have done in my life.

Now, when things happen or come up that used to send me down a negative road, I am conscious about recognizing, "This is one of my triggers," and I have the power to make a better choice. It gave me the power of the pen in writing my future!

Elina: I love that so much. So, throughout this incredible journey thus far, what has struggle, pain, and adversity taught you?

Robby: That no matter what comes my way, I am stronger! Having a growth mindset to look at every negative in my life as nothing more than an opportunity to learn something new and grow has truly been freeing. It frees me from the anxiety that I used to struggle with because I lived in fear of messing up. Now, I welcome it because I know it's going to do nothing but make me that much better.

Elina: What is something great and positive that has happened in your life recently?

Robby: For the first time in my life, I am completely comfortable with whom I am. During a recent work trip, I surrendered to my authenticity and said to myself, "On this trip, I am going to go all in on my authentic self and serve 100% of my energy from there." The trip turned out ten times better than I ever thought.

I was free and unencumbered to serve others in the highest version of myself and the connections made that weekend were incredible. It solidified to me how important this lesson is. I truly believe human potential can only be reached by giving everything you've got in service of your authentic self.

Elina: So, what's next for you? What do you see yourself accomplishing over the next five years?

Robby: I will change a million lives! I will continue my coaching business and I just launched my podcast called, *The Biohacked Life*. Through my entrepreneurial ventures, I will continue to build a business that creates a legacy of positive impact and that will allow me to make a huge impact in the lives of young people through *RISE UP*!

Elina: In closing, if you could leave the world with three lessons, what would they be?

Robby:

1. Live 100% in the service of your authentic, happy self by filling your cup first, and then, pouring from the overflow.

2. Relationships are the most important thing in the world.

3. Serve from love to be the light for everyone and do your absolute best to be the hero your friends and family need you to be.

"Every struggle you've had in your life has shaped you into the person you are today. Be thankful for the hard times, as they will only make you stronger."
– Keanu Reeves

30

The Untold: The Story of Elina Lee

"I could not have made it this far had there not been angels along the way."
– Della Reese

From the time I was fifteen until I gave birth to my son, Daniel, at the age of seventeen, is a time of my life that I haven't shared with many others yet. There are probably less than a handful of people who know what really happened. So many of my peers still ask what happened to me; they still question where I went.

This is the first time that I am openly sharing the story that so many ponder on. I've finally gathered the courage and have moved past the shame to share it in hopes that it may prevent someone from making the same mistakes that I did or inspire someone with a similar story to continue believing in themselves and fighting forward despite their circumstances.

No matter what hand life deals you, you have the choice to either take it as an opportunity to learn and grow or to take it as a hindrance and allow it to hold you back. The choice is yours. I chose to be strong for myself, clean up my act, learn from my mistakes, get on the right path, and build a positive life moving forward. You can, too. Everything and anything is possible. All you need to do is make it up in your mind. Decide what you want and what type of person you aspire to become, then don't stop until it's yours.

I was always a smart kid, always five steps ahead of my classmates, always had good grades, always did great on exams, and teachers loved me. I was great in sports, went to church, very stubborn by nature but, overall, I was a good kid growing up.

Then, thirteen happened. I went from being the smart kid to becoming the kid that parents wouldn't allow around their children. I started smoking cigarettes, marijuana, drinking beer, and skipping school which lead to me sneaking out of the house at night, going places I shouldn't have been, hanging out with juniors and seniors, dating the stereotypical douchebag football players, stealing cars, shoplifting, and getting arrested.

I became addicted to the adrenaline of being "bad." It felt so good. I was just addicted to adrenaline in general. Anything dangerous, fast, or wrong excited me. I became addicted to thrill. I climbed everything, jumped off everything, explored everything, raced cars, stole cars, experimented with drugs, dated older bad boys, snuck into nightclubs, and snuck off to other cities. I grew up fast. Way faster than everyone around me and way faster than anyone should.

My parents attempted to homeschool me. That didn't work. So, I was placed into a private religious school when I was fourteen in hopes to straighten me out. That obviously didn't work either; I just corrupted the other students. They were all so intrigued by this new girl who had a "no fucks given" attitude and left during breaks to smoke behind the school.

Unfortunately, I was expelled about a month after I was enrolled because I thought it would be entertaining to trick the kids into snorting crushed Altoids by telling them it was cocaine. It actually was quite funny; I thought so at least. The superintendent didn't think so though.

My parents placed me in another school. I followed the rules for the first month or so then I became bored and unchallenged, so I started getting back into trouble. This is when I entered the phase of stealing cars and hanging out with boys. I remember there was this one boy, in particular, who just moved in from out of state. All the girls in our school had their eyes set on him. He was this new, handsome, tall, blonde, popular, athletic football player. So, me, with my compulsive competitive nature, had to make that mine; and he was. All mine.

We took each other's virginity and spent a lot of time together. I remember wanting to see him so bad that I would sneak into my parents' room at night, open the drawer where they kept their car keys, silently take them then go back to my room to sneak out of my window, and jump the fence. I would take their brand-new sports car, put it in neutral, silently back out of the drive way and down the street before I started the engine so that they wouldn't wake up from the noise. I drove to go see him as often as I could then drove back home, snuck back in, and placed the keys in the exact position that I found them.

I remember the first time he told me he loved me. It was the most adorable thing ever. I felt so bad because he seemed so sincere and vulnerable. I replied by saying, "No, you don't." God, I was such a little insensitive asshole back then. Then, I became bored and unchallenged, so, I moved on and did my thing. Eventually, I was getting into so much trouble that my parents moved to another town and I was placed into yet another school.

I was fifteen starting a new life in a new town with new people. This was a new chance; maybe I could get it right this time, and maybe I could follow the rules for once. Wrong. This is when I started getting into the real trouble. I quit going to school a couple months after we moved, started leaving home for days and weeks at a time, experimenting with and selling drugs, shoplifting, selling stolen bottles of liquor to high school students, breaking into homes, going to parties, hanging out with college students, and living on couch to couch.

I was eventually arrested for shoplifting and placed into a juvenile correctional program on a 160-acre farm in the middle of nowhere. This place was the birth of my anger, depression, anxiety, and rage.

At the time, I didn't know that I was being sent here. We had just left a family trip to Stone Mountain in Georgia. My dad was driving, I was asleep in the front seat, and my mom and brother were in the back. The van stopped abruptly, and I woke up to a very large man pulling me out of my seat and painfully restraining my arms behind my back.

I was confused and scared. I had no idea what was happening. I didn't know where I was. Why was this man restraining me and taking me into this building? Why was my dad just standing there watching it happen?

He took me into the building and I remember him forcefully slamming my face and body into the wall. It hurt. I couldn't move. I felt like my arms were about to break because of how hard he had them pulled behind my back. He turned me around, looked me dead in the eyes, and said to me, "Get used to it. You're going to be here for a very long time."

This was a bad place. Bad things happened to the people who were sent here. No body left the same; including myself. The person that I was on June 6, 2006 (666) when I arrived was not the person that I was when I left. This place changed people, and not in a good way.

Fortunately, years later, after numerous allegations and lawsuits, it was shut down. There's no telling how many other children were abused before that day came; physically, sexually, mentally, and psychologically. This place was started in the early 1980's and wasn't closed until just a few years ago. At that age, I remember promising myself that, when I became an adult, I would become so rich and successful so that I could have the power to bring this place to an end or make an unrefusable offer to purchase the property from them. Someone beat me to it.

I remember feeling like I was sent to a prison camp. We were forced to work endless hours of physical labor outdoors in 92°-102° weather. We were forced to cook, clean, farm, mow acres of land, clean pig pens, shovel horse shit, run, do pushups, keep our uniforms clean, make our beds, and keep our areas in precise order or else we were physically punished.

I started out having a very hard time because of my stubborn and defiant nature. I've always had an issue with authority and being told what to do; I still have this issue even as an adult. It wasn't easy for me. I learned quick though. Miles and miles of running, pushup after pushup, suicide after suicide, and painful beating after painful beating will teach you to just shut the fuck up, fall in line, and obey. So, I did; for a while anyway.

Thankfully, I was never sent to "isolation" in the downstairs barracks. Some had to stay locked down there for several days at a time by themselves as a form of punishment. I was always punished physically or was forced to run. I remember one time being taken into the office and being beaten so hard by one of the staff members that I pissed myself and could barely speak.

I only saw the isolation barracks once. I remember the hall being so long, dark, and cold; all the doors were closed. It looked like a scene from a horror movie. It was the day after I was involved in a fight. They made me take a tray of food to the person that I had beaten. I was instructed to knock and leave the tray on the floor in front of her door.

I wasn't allowed to see her or speak to her since they had her in isolation, but I saw her and apologized to her anyway. I remember seeing how swollen and bruised her face was. One of her eyes were so swollen and bloody that she couldn't even open it. I couldn't believe that I did that to another human being. I was so ashamed, embarrassed, and disgusted with myself. I left her tray of food and said to myself, "I need to get the fuck out of here."

I hated the person that I was becoming being here. I know I've done illegal things prior to being here, but I wasn't an angry and violent person; not until I came here. This place does things to the people who come here. This place makes you insane. It makes you angry. It makes you afraid. It makes you see humanity in a different way. I'm sure some of the staff had good intentions for those who came here, and some may have genuinely wanted to help us, but there were others here who had no good intentions in mind.

I had only been there for just over ten weeks. It was time to devise a plan; an escape plan. Since the early 1980's, no one has ever been able to successfully escape from this place. The moment someone told me that it had never been done, I accepted the challenge. I was going to be that exception; and I was. I was the first person in history who successfully escaped this place and never had to go back.

It was set in my mind. I was getting the fuck out of here. So, I started to become more aware of my surroundings and started studying the patterns and behavior of the staff members. I listened in on their conversations, I watched silently, I paid attention to who worked what shift and what days and times to expect them. Then, it happened. I learned that the main man in charge, the fucker who beat me, was going to be leaving for a family vacation in a couple of weeks. He wasn't going to be supervising our Sunday trip into the city to clean the church.

Each Sunday, we had to go into the city to clean a church and sit through a service. Right next to the cleaning supply closet in the back of the church kitchen where no one paid any attention just so happened to be a door that led to the backside of the church building. The Sunday that he was gone, I made damn sure that I was on cleaning duty, but I couldn't do it alone. So, I had to pick and choose who I would share my plan with.

I've always had an issue trusting people; being here didn't help. I had to be very mindful and very skeptical of who I shared this plan with because I didn't want them running to tell the staff on me. The staff would probably beat me into a coma if they found out what I was trying to do. So, over the next couple of weeks, I observed, and I befriended just about every person in my building until I learned who I could trust; to an extent.

I chose three girls out of nearly twenty; two larger girls to aid as some form of protection and one bi-lingual girl to translate if needed. However, to protect myself, I didn't tell them the plan until just before it would happen. This way, even if they did tell the staff, it would be too late. I would have already been gone. Either they were in or they weren't. Didn't matter to me. I was getting out regardless.

The time came. We were finished cleaning. Myself and one of the others were heading back to the supply closet and I gave the other two a signal to follow behind. It was our moment. The staff was occupied and weren't paying attention. This was our moment. This was our window of opportunity; and we fucking took it.

I went first then the others followed right behind me. I've never ran so fast in my life. I remember running and looking to my right to see the staff yelling at the top of their lungs as they ran toward us. I pushed. I ran. I ran as hard and as fast as I fucking could. I looked back once to see if my team was behind me. Then, I just kept running.

Comically, I remember envisioning Forrest Gump running through my mind during this time. "Run, Forrest, Run!" So, I kept running. I ran until I saw an opening in the woods and we went straight in without stopping. We didn't stop until we were certain that no one was following us anymore. We lost them; finally.

Here we were in a foreign city, lost in the woods with nowhere to go, nothing to eat, no money, no identification, no plan, no phone, no one to call; nothing. But we were free and, at that time, that's all that mattered. We were free.

We kept walking in the woods until we eventually came across a trail, so, we followed the trail and it led to a State Park. By this time, it was dark, and we were starting to get anxious. I had to figure something out. I could start to hear cars passing on a road, so, we followed the noise. It led us to a very high fence that we followed and seemed to never end on either side. So, we climbed and came out on the other side. On the other side of the fence, was a neighborhood. I didn't like this. This did not feel safe.

I remember being told a story of one of the escapees who the police found in a nearby neighborhood. She also escaped on a Sunday. Unfortunately, for her, she was raped in the backyard of a nearby home before the police found her, arrested her, and returned her to the program. She was punished by staff upon her return. That's all I could envision in my mind as we walked through this neighborhood. So, I was on alert. I felt that since it was my idea to escape, I was responsible for their safety, too.

We've been walking for hours. We're drenched in sweat; all in uniform. We're hungry, exhausted, dehydrated, and lost. We eventually see someone walking ahead. We approach him to ask if we can use his phone. He doesn't speak much English, so, one of the girls translates and he eventually lets us use his phone after much speculation. There was only one person who I felt that I could call at that time, but it was a dead end.

The man starts questioning who we are, where we came from, and why we were all dressed the exact same. So, we told him the truth. He was shocked but, surprisingly, offered to help and let us come inside to get out of the rain.

At this point, we're all on edge and watching this man's every move in case he tries something. Then, the door opens and in walks this very large man covered in tattoos with a shaved head wearing a white wife-beater. He was just released from prison the day prior. Now, we're definitely on edge. He pulls out a bag of cocaine and drops it on the table in front of us.

The other man is on the phone speaking Spanish. We're watching his every move and are ready to run at any given moment. He walks over and tells us that he called his brother who has a home in the country where we could stay until we came up with a plan.

I wasn't comfortable with this. I assumed that there had to be an ulterior motive. Why would a stranger want to help us? But, in this situation, we had nowhere else to go or anyone else to turn to, so we accepted his offer.

I remember paying attention to each turn, street sign, landmark, and building along the way so that we could find our way back if we needed to escape again. We arrived and met his brother. He was an older gentleman, very kind, timid, shy, quiet, and kept his word. We stayed in his home safe, fed, and unharmed for the next two days.

On the third morning, they suggested that we start coming up with a plan to get in contact with our parents. The other girls were terrified to reach out to theirs, so, we went to mine. I was too nervous to call them on the phone and I was also afraid that they would notify the police of our location. So, instead, we went straight to them; in person.

One of the girls didn't want to leave because she didn't feel safe going to my parents. She wanted to stay there. I remember trying so hard to convince her to come with us, but she refused. So, we had no choice but to leave her behind. The men paid for a rental car, drove us to my parents' home nearly eight hours away, and never asked for anything in return. Unfortunately, the police received an anonymous call and they came to the home the next day, arrested the girl who stayed, and immediately returned her to the program.

When we arrived at my parents' home, I remember feeling so anxious and afraid as I walked up to the front door and rang the doorbell. I wanted to let them know days ago that I was safe, but I had a feeling not to. This was the right way. My dad answers the door and immediately holds me, and we start crying. I tell him what happened during the program, where we were, and how these men generously helped us get home. We were finally safe. We were finally home.

Unfortunately, the police eventually came to arrest the two girls that were with me and returned them to the program. After sharing my story with my parents, they refused to let the police take me back to the program. Instead, I was fortunate enough to have the opportunity to return to court, serve community service, attend regular counseling sessions, and check in frequently with a probation officer.

Before the men left after bringing us to my parents' home, we went to the car to thank them again. All this time, I didn't know the man's name who had been so selfless, generous, and eager to help us. So, I asked him, and he replied in an accent, "My name is Ángel. It means *'Angel'* in English."

He was my Angel. He saved me. Because of him, I was able to start a new life and become the woman I am today.

"*All God's angels come to us disguised.*"
– James Russel Lowell

About the Author

From getting arrested as an adolescent, dropping out of school, becoming a mother at seventeen, surviving sexual abuse, depression and anxiety, making millions then walking away from it all; Elina's story is a perfect example of how anyone can achieve success despite their circumstances.

Full-time mother. Mental health advocate. Self-made millionaire. High school and college drop-out. Adrenaline junkie. Bad ass. Just a few words to describe her. Since she was a child, Elina was never afraid of risk or a challenge; in fact, she has always embraced it, welcomed it, and searched for it.

She started her first company at age twenty when she dropped out of college where she had her eyes set on becoming a doctor. Life had other plans for her. During this time, Elina was a broke, full-time student, and single mother caring for her son on her own. Although she had plans to become a doctor, she still wasn't exactly sure of what she wanted to do with her life; all she knew was that, one day, she wanted to become successful, empower, help, and inspire others.

Fast forward a couple years and she helped to build a multi-million-dollar industry from a broken laptop that she used on someone else's kitchen table while living on a mattress behind someone else's couch. During this time, she helped to produce nearly five hundred events in ten different countries and her companies have been featured in countless magazines, news outlets, television appearances, and publications around the world.

For years, all the success, traveling, and busy non-stop schedules distracted her from what she knew was of true importance and value: happiness, family, love, and inner-peace.

After privately and quietly battling with depression, anxiety, and an unhappy marriage for nearly a decade, she finally gathered the courage to stand up for herself and leave everything behind, including the successful companies that she loved and helped build in order to embark on her personal journey toward inner-success, writing her first book, and starting a new company that absolutely sets her soul on fire.

With nearly ten years of experience in event production, she is overjoyed to be passionately working on The Inner Success Project's *Cruises, Life Mastery Retreats,* and *Success Coaching Programs.*

Her mission and vision for these events, which take place four times each year in different countries around the world, is to create a community and place for positive, like-minded people to gather, grow, empower and support one another while traveling the world, as well as, to create a solid platform for motivational keynote speakers, life coaches, and "come-ups" to share their stories through her *#SHAREYOURSTORY* project.

Each *ISP Cruise* and *Life Mastery Retreat* features exciting daily and nightly themed events, charity galas, soirees, adventures, group excursions (like kayaking, zip lining, ATVing, cave diving, hiking, etc.), group activities, workouts, workshops, and so much more! And, better yet; each of her events are family friendly so the kids can come along!

Her *ISP Success Coaching Programs* are led by Certified and Professional "Results Coaches" around the country. Each one-on-one program, in-person program, and online program is individually customized and designed by an ISP Success Coach to fit the needs, goals, and visions of the client in any area from "health and fitness" to "business and finance" to "personal growth and development" to "marriage and relationships;" and more.

Today, Elina spends her days enjoying the life that truly makes her happy: coaching, empowering, and inspiring others, writing, focusing on her physical, mental, emotional, and spiritual development, hiking, exploring, traveling, and spending quality time with her son, family, and loved ones.

"Inner peace is the new success."
– DaVida Rowley

For more information on how you can attend
The Inner Success Project's *Cruises* and *Life Mastery Retreats* or to apply for a "One-on-One" *Success Coaching Program* with Elina or any of our Certified ISP Coaches, call 1-800-213-1302 or visit

www.innersuccessproject.com

CPSIA information can be obtained
at www.ICGtesting.com
Printed in the USA
BVHW031231200519
548789BV00012B/1357/P

9 780578 418650